AFTER DEATH

A PERSONAL NARRATIVE
ENLARGED EDITION
OF

LETTERS FROM JULIA

AFTER DEATH

A PERSONAL NARRATIVE
ENLARGED EDITION
OF

LETTERS FROM JULIA

W. T. STEAD

After Death or Letters from Julia

White Crow Books is an imprint of
White Crow Productions Ltd
PO Box 1013
Guildford
GU1 9EJ

www.whitecrowbooks.com

Text design and eBook production by Essential Works
www.essentialworks.co.uk

eBook ISBN 978-907355-90-5

Body, Mind, Spirit/Spiritualism

Distributed in the UK by
Lightning Source Ltd.
Chapter House
Pitfield
Kiln Farm
Milton Keynes MK11 3LW

Distributed in the USA by
Lightning Source Inc.
246 Heil Quaker Boulevard
LaVergne
Tennessee 37086

Contents

Preface   6

Introduction   12

First Series – To Her Friend   19

    Crossing the Bar   20

    The Surprises of the New Life   26

    On the Bliss of Heaven   32

    On Mourning for the Dead   36

    The Law of Spiritual Growth   41

Second Series – To the Writer   47

    After the Border Has Been Crossed   48

    Life on the Other Side   61

    How to Widen the Chinks   77

    The Use and Abuse of Spirit Communications   91

    The Open Door to the Open Secret   107

    On the Losing and the Finding of the Soul   122

    Parting Words   130

Fragments   137

Appendix   143

Preface

EIGHT YEARS AGO I collected together and published the series of messages contained in this volume under the title, *Letters from Julia, or Light from the Borderland, received by automatic writing from one who has as gone before.* Since then the little volume has been six times reprinted in England, and at least one translation has appeared abroad. I have received so many grateful letters from persons in all parts of the world, who, after sorrowing for their dead as those that have no hope, felt on reading this book as if their lost ones were in very truth restored to life, that I can no longer refuse to issue it to a wider public. I have not changed a word or syllable in the letters themselves. They stand exactly as they were printed in the original edition where they were reproduced from the automatic manuscript of the invisible author who used my passive hand as her amanuensis. I have also left unaltered the introduction explaining how these letters were written. But I have changed the title to one which is more challenging than "Letters from Julia", and which also indicates more explicitly the subject of the book.

It may save me some unnecessary correspondence if, when introducing this new edition of the communications received from my friend Miss Julia who "what we call died" on December 12, 1891, I state once for all that the narrative given in the preface is a simple statement of fact. There is no "dressing" of any kind. The friend whom I call Ellen is still alive. Miss Julia was well known to many who are conspicuous in good works on both sides of the Atlantic. Many persist in regarding the name Julia as if it were some fantastic appellation given to an imaginary entity. It was simply the Christian name given to my friend in infancy when she was baptized, and as she was known by it while in her former body, her friends continue to call her by the same name. There is no more reason for changing one's name because we change bodies than when we change dresses. I would have no hesitation about giving my friend's full name with all particulars as to her life history, were it not for two reasons. Some of her relatives might object, and if I published her full name I should deprive myself at once of a very simple test, first, as to the non-authenticity of messages professing to come from pseudo "Julias," and secondly, as to the futility of the popular delusion that psychic messages are always to be explained by thought transference. Her name is, of course, perfectly familiar to me, but in a dozen years, out of scores of psychics and mediums of all kinds, all of whom on the telepathic hypothesis ought to have had no difficulty in reading her name in my mind, only two have ever been able to tell me her surname.

I have not one word to alter or to modify in the statement made in the original preface, where I vouch for my absolute belief in the authenticity of the communications received through my hand. I am positive that the letters did not proceed from my conscious mind. Of my unconscious mind I am, of course, unconscious. But I can hardly imagine that any part of my unconscious self would deliberately practice a hoax upon my conscious self about the most serious of all subjects, and keep it up year after year with the utmost apparent sincerity and consistency. The simple explanation that my friend who has passed over can use my hand as her own seems much more natural and probable. I have many friends who, being still in their bodies, can write with my hand automatically at any distance. If this capacity be inherent in the soul of man, independent of the body, when incarnate in flesh, why should it perish when the bodily vesture is laid aside like a worn-out garment? Automatic telepathic writing received from those whom we call living persons does not prove that similar communications can take place after one of these persons has put on immortality. But as it accustoms us to a mode of communicating thoughts without any conscious or visible use of the body of the communicator, it does away with the chief obstacle to the acceptance of messages from those whose physical bodies are mouldering in the dust. If my friends' minds do not need to use their own hands to write to me but can control my hand for that purpose while they are still in the physical body, why should they lose that faculty merely because they have put on a spiritual body? It is not their material envelope that writes with my hand at a distance of hundreds, or even thousands of miles, but a subtler something that is quite independent of their body and even their physical consciousness.

As to the salient truth asserted in these messages, the return of one from beyond the grave to inform those who remain behind of the life beyond, and of the light which the other world sheds upon this, I can only say that I believe it to be true. Those who reply by quoting Shakespeare's saying about the bourne from which no traveler e'er returns, may be disposed of by the remark that Shakespeare himself was of a different opinion. If that saying be true, the Christian religion is based on falsehood, and not the Christian religion alone. The reminder, recently afforded, that to the Japanese the constant and conscious presence of the spirits of the departed is as much a reality of their everyday, work-a-day existence as their artillery and ironclads, may do something to reconcile some of our superior latter day Christians to a reassertion of one of the fundamental truths of the faith in which they profess to believe. When my friend describes her own experiences after death, I accept her statements as I accepted her description of what she saw at Ober Ammergau the year before she died. She was always a truthful woman, and I don't think that the change called death was likely to impair her veracity. At the same time I do not for a moment believe that her experiences are to be accepted as those common to all the departed. "In my Father's house are many mansions," and each soul goes to its own place.

Apart from what is peculiar or personal to herself, two or three things common to all appear to be clearly asserted in these messages. The first is that death makes no break in the continuity of mental consciousness. Our personality persists with so vivid a sense of its own identity that there is often at first some difficulty in realizing that death has taken place. The second is that the period of growth and probation is no more complete at death than it is on leaving school, finishing an apprenticeship, or retiring from business. The environment is changed. But the principle of growth, of evolution, of endless progress toward ideal perfection, continues to be the law of life. The third is that it is not only possible but lawful, and not only lawful, but an absolute duty on the part of mortals to renew and keep up a loving intercourse with the loved ones who have gone before. Such an imperious duty imposed by the loving heart is not to be thrust on one side by quoting inapplicable texts by which the Hebrew lawgiver three thousand years ago sought to deter the children of Israel from resorting to familiar spirits, and the black magic of primitive times. As earnestly as any writer in the Pentateuch I raise my voice against any tampering with the unseen and potent spirits of evil which lie in wait for the soul. But our friends do not become evil demons merely because they have changed their bodily raiment. Of this let readers of these message from beyond the grave form their own opinion.

It may be asked why, if this be the case, I have done nothing to establish the Bureau of which my friend writes so much. I have been willing, but I have not felt the imperious call which impels me to thrust aside all obstacles and say it must be done. I am a public man, immersed in public affairs, and I have felt that call in relation to mundane things, which left me neither means nor leisure to attempt to found the Bureau. If any who read this book feel called to co-operate in such an effort, I shall be very glad to hear from them, if they have any practical suggestions to make or help to offer.

I am often asked if I still hear from my friend. I am glad to say that there has been no break in the intimacy of our relations. I have a mass of other messages, which some day I may sift out and publish. But the letters contained in this little book are complete in themselves. I asked my friend before writing these last sentences if she had anything to say. Using my hand as she has ever done she wrote:

"I have only to add one word more.

"All that I have written is true and good. I have nothing to alter. With all that I have much more to say that I do not say now. These years, which to you seem so long, to me have been but as the gleaming joy of a summer's day. You will go on and you will see how true is all that I have said. As to the Bureau, I am as strong for it as ever. But perhaps I was wrong in urging you to undertake its organization. There are others with more leisure and more means. But I still feel that although others may provide the means and undertake the management, you are called from this side to see that the Bureau is established.

"The one thing more that I would like to add is this:

"All that I wrote about the joy and the glory of the Love of God, which is manifested to us more and more exceedingly, was too weak, too poor to give you any idea of how Life becomes, transfigured when the atmosphere of Life is Love. – Julia."

WILLIAM T. STEAD
MOSCOW, OCTOBER 10, 1905

Introduction

J ULIA AND ELLEN, two women in the prime of their years, were united by a lifelong friendship which not even death was strong enough to sever. They were both devout Christians, more absorbed in good works for the living than in speculations about the dead. But when at times the tomb cast its chill shadow across their busy lives they would renew the pledge so familiar to those whose love overleaps the barrier of the grave, and would again exchange the solemn covenant that whoever was taken first would, if it were permitted, return to the other who was left, and keep a solemn tryst. The visible manifestation of that actual presence of the departed would thus banish all doubt and convince the survivor as to the uninterrupted continuance of both life and love beyond the grave.

The years passed on. Julia died. The blow of the bereavement fell heavily upon all her friends, but upon none so cruelly as upon Ellen. The light of her life seemed to have gone out in the blackness of the darkness of death. For some months it seemed as if existence without her friend was a burden too great to be borne.

But one night the promise was fulfilled. Ellen was sleeping in her old home, when suddenly she was waked up. It was night, but the room was full of light. And close to her bedside she saw Julia in her habit as she lived, radiant with life and peace and joy. She had redeemed her promise. For some moments she stood there, smiling but silent. Ellen was too awestruck to speak. The sudden and unmistakable fulfillment of the desire of her heart seemed to rob her of all her faculty but that of feeling unspeakable joy. Then the figure slowly, almost imperceptibly dissolved away, and Ellen was once more alone.

Several months later Ellen visited this country, and again Julia fulfilled her covenant and kept her promised tryst. I happened to be staying in the same country house, and as I had known Julia, and was interested in such matters, Ellen told me the story of these two visits. After describing how Julia came the first time, she continued: "I saw her again the other night, in my room there. In both cases I saw her in the same way. I was sleeping. I was suddenly woken up, and saw her standing by my bedside. Then she faded away, and I only saw the light in the place where she had been standing. The first time, I thought it might have been a hallucination, as her death was recent, and I was in such terrible distress about her; but the other night there was no mistake about it. I saw her quite distinctly. I know it was Julia, and she has come back to me as she promised. But I could not hear her speak, and I cannot bear to think that she may have come back with a message for me, and yet I could not hear what she had to say."

As I had at that time – much to my own surprise – begun to develop a hitherto unsuspected gift of automatic writing, I offered, in case she were willing and able to use my hand as her own, to allow Julia to write what message she pleased by that means.

Automatic writing, I may explain for those unfamiliar with the term, is writing that is written by the hand of a person which is not under control of his conscious mind. The hand apparently writes of itself, the person to whom the hand belongs having no knowledge of what it is about to write. It is a very familiar and simple form of mediumship, which in no way impairs the writer's faculties or places his personality under the control of any other intelligence. This writing may proceed from his sub-conscious mind, or it may be due to the direct action of independent, invisible intelligences. What is certain is that it does not emanate from the conscious mind of the writer, who often receives messages containing information as to past events of which he has never heard, and sometimes perfectly accurate predictions as to events which have not yet happened.

It was in this way that I began to receive the communications, some few of which are collected in this little volume. I received all the "Letters from Julia" in the same manner. Sitting alone with a tranquil mind, I consciously placed my right hand, with the pen held in the ordinary way, at the disposal of Julia, and watched with keen and skeptical interest to see what it would write. The bulk of the first series was written as letters from Julia to Ellen. They were written as from one friend to another, beginning and ending just as if the writer were still in the body instead of having to rely upon the loan of my hand. The second series was written for publication at irregular intervals. The first series is really a compost of extracts, from letters which were written every week for nearly six months, with some intercalated observations made to me at the time of writing. The second series is composed of the communications written as printed at the dates given in the text. The reader will probably regret the continual interruption of the narrative by the interpolated objections and questions printed in italics. On reflection, however, he will probably agree that the reproduction of the letters just as they were received, with the contemporary record of the thoughts of the conscious mind of the writer, whose hand was the unconscious agent for their transmission, was necessary, if only in order to show how far it is from the truth to assert that the Julia letters were the outcome of my conscious mind.

It is not necessary for me to enter into a detailed statement of the evidence which has led me to the conclusion that these "Letters from Julia" are really what they profess to be – communications from the disembodied spirit of one who was my friend in her earth- life, but whose friendship has been far closer and more real to me since she was taken from us six years ago.

The evidence may be briefly summarized under the following heads:

1 The beginning of the communications as above described.

2 The giving of a test in the first message of an affectionate *sobriquet* bestowed by her on her death bed, which was known to her friend but unknown to me.

3 The minute description of an incident which had occurred in or about 1885, of which I had never heard, and which Ellen herself had entirely forgotten until her memory was revived by the mention of details of place and time, which were quite unknown to me.

4 The writing out with my hand of names, Christian and surname, entirely unknown to me, who were her friends in her native land.

5 The intense personal and affectionate interest taken by the user of my hand in persons and movements in which my interest was by no means so deep as was Julia's.

6 The strongly marked and unvarying personal idio-
syncrasy of the writer of these Letters, which is certainly not my own – is, I am afraid, in many respects
very much superior to my own.

In addition to these internal evidences, there was the evidence of psychic persons gifted with the power of seeing the spiritual forms that surround all of us. To those
who deny that such forms exist, or are visible to anyone,
this evidence naturally does not count. But even those
skeptics would probably weaken in their dogmatic incre-
dulity if, after accompanying me to seer after seer, persons to whom I was totally unknown either by name or
by features, they were to find that each and all of these
gifted with psychic vision described, among others, the
easily recognizable form of Julia. Those who know that
certain persons have this gift of clear seeing will realize
my increased sense of the objective reality of her presence when I state the following facts:

1 That strangers who have never heard of her existence
have described her as standing near me when my automatic hand was writing.

2 That several of them have not only described her but
have given her name.

3 That one here and one in her native land have also
given her surname, which I have refrained from publishing, and which I have equally in vain endeavored
to telepath to the minds of other mediums.

4 That in one case the seer picked Julia's portrait out of
a score, from which there was nothing to distinguish
it, and identified it as "the lady who writes with" me.

5 That in another case details were given in the

description by the seer which I believed and asserted were mistaken, but which, on reference to her more intimate friends, were admitted to be correct;

6 And that by arrangement, Julia has kept appointments with seers at great distances from me.

Besides these reasons for believing that the intelligence which moved my hand when the "Letters from Julia" were written is not my own, but a superior intelligence independent of my work-a-day consciousness, there is the fact that on several occasions she has foretold with no less persistence than accuracy events which did not happen for months, and which I roundly told her I did not believe could possibly happen.

Hence I feel it impossible to resist the conclusion that these communications are what they profess to be – real letters from the real Julia, who is not dead but gone before. I know, after five years' almost daily intercourse with her through my automatic hand, that I am conversing with an intelligence, at least as keen as my own, a personality as distinctly defined and a friend as true and tender, as I have ever known. From those who scout the possibility of such a phenomenon I would merely ask the admission that in this case their favorite theory of intentional fraud, at least on the part of the medium, is excluded by the fact that these messages were written by my own right hand, no other visible person being present. No one who knows anything of the prejudice that exists on the subject will deny that I have no personal interest to serve in taking up the exceedingly unpopular and much ridiculed position of a believer in the reality of such communications. For years I have labored under a serious disadvantage on this account in many ways, both private and public. I am well aware that the contents of this Preface will be employed in order to discount and discredit everything I may do or say for years to come. That is unfortunate, no doubt, but of course it cannot be weighed in the balance compared with the importance of testifying to what I believe to be the truth about the messages written with my hand.

In conclusion, I have only to say that, while the source of these messages is of course a matter of the first importance in so far as they bear testimony to things not within human ken, the intrinsic value of three-fourths of the "Letters from Julia" is no more dependent upon theories as to their origin than the merits of Shakespeare's plays depend upon theories of their authorship. Grant, if you will, that the Letters were written solely by my subconscious self, that would in no way impair the truth or diminish the force of these eloquent and touching pleas for the Higher Life. I only wish my conscious self could write so well.

These "Letters" are partially made up from extracts from letters written with my hand, by Julia to her friend Ellen in 1892–3, together with others addressed to me. As these grew out of the correspondence with Ellen, I have included them in the first series. The letter headings are, of course, my own.

W. T. STEAD
MOWBRAY HOUSE, TEMPLE, W. C.
CHRISTMAS, 1897

FIRST SERIES – TO HER FRIEND

1

Crossing the Bar

When I left you, darling, you thought I was gone from you forever, or at least till you also passed over. But I was never so near to you as after I had, what you called, died.

How You Feel After Death
I found myself free from my body. It was such a strange new feeling. I was standing close to the bedside on which my body was lying; I saw every as thing in the room just as before I closed my eyes.

How She Felt In Dying
I did not feel any pain in "dying;" I felt only a great calm and peace. Then I awoke, and I was standing outside my old body, in the room. There was no one there at first, just myself and my old body. At first I wondered I was so strangely well. Then I saw that I had passed over.

I waited about a little: then the door opened and Mrs. H. came in. She was very sad; she addressed my poor body as if it was, myself. I was standing looking at her, but all her thoughts were upon the poor old body I had left behind. It seemed so absurd I could not help laughing. I did not try to speak at first; I waited to see what would happen.

An Angel and Her Mission
Then I felt as though a great warm flood of light had

come into the room, and I saw an angel. She, for at first she seemed to be a female, came to me and said:

"I am sent to teach you the laws of the new life."

And as I looked, she gently touched me and said: "We must go."

Then I left the room and my poor old body, and passed out. It was so strange; the streets were full of spirits. I could see them as we passed; they seemed to be just like ourselves. My angel had wings; they were very beautiful. She was all robed in white.

We went at first through the streets, then we went through the air, till we came to the place where we met friends who had passed on before.

Reunion and Separation

There were Mr. M.— , and Mr. M.— and Ethel A.—, and many others. They told me much about the spirit world. They said I must learn its laws, and endeavor to be as useful as I could. The angel who remained with me all the time helped me to explain.

The spirit friends had their life much as it was here; they lived and loved, and if they had not to work for their daily bread, they had still plenty to do.

Return to Friends

Then I began to be sad about you, and I wanted to go back; the angel took me swiftly through the air to where I came from. When I entered the death-chamber there lay my body. It was no longer of interest to me, but I was so grieved to see how you were all weeping over my worn-out clothes, I wished to speak to you. I saw you, darling, all wet with tears, and I was so sad I could not cheer you.

The Veil Not Yet Drawn Back

I very much wanted to speak and tell you how near I was to you, but I could not make you hear.

I tried, but you took no notice of me. I said to the angel:

"Will it be always thus?"

She said, "Wait; the time will come when you will speak with her. But at present she cannot hear, neither can she understand."

The Voice of the Invisible

I was then called away. I found myself in a great expanse of landscape where I had never been before. I was alone; that is, I saw no one. But you are never really alone. We are always living in the presence of God. But I saw no one. Then I heard a voice. I did not see whence it came, or who spoke. I only heard the words, "Julia, *He who saved thee would fain speak with thee.*" I listened, but no words other than these were spoken.

The Flame-Bright One

Then I said, "Who is it that speaks?" And, behold, a flaming fire – really like fire, though in human shape. I was afraid. Then he spoke and said, "Be not afraid. It is I, who am appointed to teach thee the secret things of God." Then I saw that the brightness as of fire was only the brightness that comes from the radiant love of the Immortals.

"Behold Your Savior"

Then the flame-bright one said to me, "Julia, behold your Savior!" and when I looked I saw Him. He was sitting on a seat close to me, and He said, "Beloved, in my Father's House are many mansions; here am I whom you have loved so long. I have prepared a place for you."

And I said, "Where, oh, my Lord?" He smiled, and in the brightness of that smile I saw the whole landscape change as the Alps change in the sunset, which I saw so often from the windows of my hotel at Lucerne. Then I saw that I was not alone, but all around and above were fair and loving forms, some of those whom I had known, others of whom I had heard, while some were strange. But all were friends, and the air was full of love. And in the midst of all was He, my Lord and Savior. He was as a Man among men. He was full of the wonderful sweet mildness which you are acquainted with in some of the pictures that have been painted by the Italian Fra Angelico. He had an admirable look of, warm affection, which was as the very breath of life to my soul. He is with us always.

Heaven Defined

This is Heaven – to be with Him. You cannot understand how the consciousness of His presence makes the atmosphere of this world so different from that with you. There are many things I wish I could write to you, but I cannot, nor could you understand them. I can only tell you that He is more than we have ever imagined. He is the Source and Giver of all good gifts. All that we know of what is good, and sweet, and noble, and lovable are but faint reflections of the immensity of the glory that is His. And He loves us with such tender love!

The Love of Jesus

Oh, Ellen, Ellen, you and I used to love each other with what seemed to us sometimes too deep and intense a love, but that at its very best was but the pale reflection of the love with which He loves us, which is marvelously and wonderfully great beyond all power of mind to describe. His name is Love; it is what He is – Love, Love, Love!

I cannot tell you everything; you could not understand it. But I am in a state of bliss such as we never imagined when on earth. I am with my friends who went before.

The Raiment of Immortal Youth

No one seems to be old. We are young, with what seems to be immortal youth. We can, when we please, assume the old bodies or their spiritual counterparts as we can assume our old clothes for purposes of identification, but our spiritual bodies here are young and beautiful. There is a semblance between what we are and what we were. We might recognize the new by its likeness to the old, but it is very different. The disembodied soul soon assumes the new raiment of youth, from which all decay has been removed.

The Life Beyond

I find it so difficult to explain how we live, and how we spend our time. We never weary, and do not need to sleep as we did on earth; neither do we need to eat or drink; these things were necessary for the material body; here we do not need them. I think we can best teach you what we experience by asking you to remember those moments of exaltation when, in the light of the setting or rising sun, you look out, happy and contented, upon the landscape over which the sun's rays have shed their magical beauty. There is peace; there is life; there is beauty; above all, there is love. Beauty everywhere, joy and love. Love, love is the secret of Heaven. God is love, and when you are lost in love you are found in God.

How Sin Appears to Her

You ask me what we feel about the sin and sorrow of the world. We reply that we see it, and seek to remove it. But it does not oppress us as it used to do, for we see the other side. We cannot doubt the love of God. We live in it. It is the greatest, the only real thing. The sins and sorrows of the earth-life are but as shadows that will flee away. But they are not merely on the earth plane; there is sin and there is sorrow on this side.

Hell, and the Joy of Heaven

Hell is on this side as well as Heaven. But it is the joy of Heaven to be always emptying Hell.

We are learning always to save by love, how to redeem by sacrifice. We must make sacrifices; otherwise there is no salvation. What else is the secret of Christ?

2

The Surprises of the New Life

While my hand was writing a letter to Ellen I thought, "I wonder if the new life surprised Julia much." Instantly she wrote:

Yes, I was not prepared for such oneness in the life on both sides.

The Soul After Death

When the soul leaves the body it remains exactly the same as when it was in the body; the soul, which is the only real self, and which uses the mind and the body as its instruments, no longer has the use or the need of the body. But it retains the mind, knowledge, experience, the habits of thought, the inclinations; they remain exactly as they were. Only it often happens that the gradual decay of the fleshy envelope to some extent obscures and impairs the real self which is liberated by death.

The Real Self

The most extraordinary thing which came to my knowledge when I passed over was the difference between the apparent man and the real self.

How We Are Judged

It gave quite a new meaning to the warning; "Judge not," for the real self is built up even more by the use it makes of the mind than by the use it makes of the body. There are here men who seemed to be vile and filthy to their fellows, who are far, far, far superior, even in purity and holiness, to men who in life kept an outward veneer of apparent goodness while the mind rioted in all wantonness. It is the mind that makes character.

It is the mind that is far more active, more potent than the body, which is but a poor instrument at best. Hence the thoughts and intents of the heart, the imaginations of the mind, these are the things by which we are judged; for it is they which make up and create, as it were, the real character of the inner self, which becomes visible after the leaving of the body.

The Power of Thought

Thought has much greater reality than you imagine. The day- dreamer is not so idle as you imagine. The influence of his idealizing speculation may not make him work, but it may be felt imperceptibly by more practical minds. And so, in like manner, the man – who in his innermost heart gives himself up to evil and unclean thoughts may be generating forces, the evil influences of which stir the passions and ruin the lives, it may be, of his own children, who possibly never knew that their father had ever had a thought of sin.

The Thoughts and Intents of the Heart

Hence on this side things seem so topsy-turvy. The first are last, the last first. I see convicts and murderers and adulterers, who worked their wickedness out in the material sphere, standing far higher in the scale of purity and of holiness than some who never committed a crime, but whose minds, as it were, were the factory and breeding-ground of thoughts which are the seed of crimes in others. I do not mean by this that it is better to do crimes than to think them. Only that the doing is not always to be taken as proof of wicked-heartedness. The sins of impulse, the crimes perpetrated in a gust of passion – these harm the soul less and do less harm than the long indulged thoughts of evil which come at last to poison the whole soul.

When the body is cast off the real state of the case is visible. Then it is for the first time that we are seen as we really are or rather have been thinking. The revelation is startling, and even now I am but dimly beginning to be accustomed to it.

The Nothingness of Things

Then there is another thing that surprised me not a little, and that was, or is, the discovery of the nothingness of things. I mean that the entire nothingness of most things which seemed to one on earth the most important things. For instance, money, rank, worth, merit, station, and all the things we most prize when on earth, are simply nothing. They don't exist any more than the mist of yesterday or the weather of last year. They were no doubt influential for a time, but they do not last; they pass as the cloud passes, and are not visible any more.

An Appeal for Help

I want to ask you if you can help me at all in a matter in which I am much interested. I have long wanted to establish a place where those who have passed over could communicate with the loved ones behind. At present the world is full of spirits longing to speak to those from whom they have been parted, just as I longed to speak to you, but without finding a hand to enable them to write. It is a strange spectacle. On your side, souls full of anguish for bereavement; on this side, souls full of sadness because they cannot communicate with those whom they love. What can be done to bring these sombre, sorrow-laden persons together? To do so requires something which we cannot supply.

The Sting of Death

You must help. But how? It is not impossible. And when it is done death will have lost its sting and the grave its victory. The apostle thought this was done. But the grave has not been so easily defeated, and death keeps its sting. Who can console us for the loss of our beloved? Only those who can show that they are not lost but are with us more than ever. Do you not think I have been much more with Ellen since I put off my flesh than I used to be? Why, I dwell with her in a way that before was quite impossible. I was never more with her than I have been since I came to this side. But she would not have known it, nor would you have heard from me at all but for the accident of your meeting.

Wanted, a Bureau of Communication

What is wanted is a bureau of communication between the two sides. Could you not establish some such sort of office with one or more trust worthy mediums? If only it were to enable the sorrowing on earth to know, if only for once, that their so-called dead live nearer them than ever before, it would help to dry many a tear and soothe many a sorrow. I think you could count upon the co-operation of all on this side.

We on this side are full of joy at the hope of this coming to pass. Imagine how grieved we must be to see so many whom we love, sorrowing without hope, when those for whom they sorrow are trying in vain every means to make them conscious of their presence. And many also are racked with agony, imagining that their loved ones are lost in hell, when in reality they have been found in the all-embracing arms of the love of God. Ellen, dear, do talk of this with Minerva, and see what can be done. It is the most important thing there is to do. For it brings with it the trump of the Archangel, when those that were in their graves shall awake and walk forth once more among men.

A Spiritual Revival

I was at first astonished to learn how much importance the spirits attach to the communications which they are allowed to have with those on earth. I can, of course, easily understand, because I feel it myself – the craving there is to speak to those whom you loved and whom you but it is much more than this. What they tell me on all sides, and especially my dear guides, is that the time is come when there is to be a great spiritual awakening among the nations, and that the agency which is to bring this about is the sudden and conclusive demonstration, in every individual case which seeks for it, of the reality of the spirit, of the permanence of the soul, and the immanence of the Divine. I said: *"But how can I help?"*

She wrote: "You are a good writing medium. If you would allow your hand to be used by the spirit of any on this side whose relatives or friends wished to hear from them, you could depend almost confidently upon the spirit using your hand. At any rate, I could always explain why they could use your hand."

3

On the Bliss of Heaven

The Difference Between Heaven and Earth

On another occasion I asked her, "What is it, for instance, which makes heaven so much better than earth?" She wrote: There are degrees in Heaven. And the lowest heaven is higher than the most wonderful vision of its bliss that you ever had. There is nothing to which you can compare our constantly loving state in this world except the supreme beatitude of the lover who is perfectly satisfied with and perfectly enraptured with the one whom he loves. For the whole difference between this side and your side consists in this – without entering now into the question of body and matter – that we live in love, which is God, and you too often live in the misery which is the natural, necessary result of the absence of God, who is love.

The Secret of World Saving

There is much love on earth. Were it not so it would be hell. There is the love of the mother for her children; of brother and sister; of young man and maiden; of husband and wife; of friends, whether men or women, or whether the friendship is between those of the same sex. All these forms of love are the rays of heaven in earth. They are none of them complete. They are the sparkling light from the diamond facets, the totality of which is God. The meanest man or woman who loves is, so far as they love, inspired by the Divine. The whole secret of the saving of the world lies in that – you must have more love – more love – more love.

Love is Self-Sacrifice

You may say that there is a love which is selfish and a love which is evil. It is true, but that is because the love is imperfect. It is not love when it leads to selfishness. The love which leads a mother to engross herself with her own children and neglect all her duties to other people is not wrong itself. It is only because she has not love enough for others that her love for her children makes her selfish. The great need wherever love seems to make people selfish is not less love for those whom they do love, but more love for the others who are neglected. You never love anyone too much. It is only that we don't love others enough also.

The Divine Ideal

Perfect love all around is the Divine ideal, and when love fails at any point, then evil is in danger of coining in. But even guilty love, so far as it takes you out of yourself, and makes you toil, and pray, and live, and perhaps die for the man or woman whom you should never have loved, brings you nearer Heaven than selfish, loveless marriage. I do not say this as against marriage. I know you think that this is dangerous doctrine. All true doctrine is dangerous, but is not less true for its danger. There is no doubt that much so- called love is very selfish, and is not love at all. The love, for instance, which leads a man to ruin a woman, and desert her when he has gratified a temporary passion, is not love. It is not easy to distinguish it from the deadliest hate. It is self- indulgence in its worst shape. Now, all love is of the nature of self- sacrifice. There are many things also to be borne in mind. We have all not merely to think what is the result to ourselves, but also to other persons, some of whom may not yet be born.

What True Love Means
To love, therefore, anyone really, truly, means that we are putting ourselves in his place, loving him as ourselves; that we desire for him the best, and give up ourselves and our own pleasure in order to secure it for him. This is true love, and wherever you find it you find a spark of God. That is why mothers are so much nearer God than anyone else. They love more – that is, they are more like God; it is they who keep the earth from becoming a vast hell.

God is Love
Now, my darling, hold fast to this central doctrine: Love is God, God is Love. The more you love, the more you are like God. It is only when we deeply, truly love, we find our true selves, or that we see the Divine in the person loved. O Ellen, Ellen! If I could come back and speak in the ears or the children of men, I think I should wish to say nothing but this – Love! Love is the fulfilling of the law; love is the seeing of the face of God. Love is God, God is Love. If you wish to be with God – love. If you wish to be in heaven – love! For Heaven differs chiefly from earth and from hell in that in heaven all love up to the full measure of their being, and all growth in grace is growth in love.

34

The Alpha and the Omega

Love! Love! Love! That is the first word and the last word. There is none beside that, for God, who is love, is all, in all, the Alpha and the Omega, the first and the last, world without end. Oh, my darling Ellen, this is indeed a true word. It is the Word which the world needs; it is the Word which became flesh and dwelt amongst men – Love, love, love!

4

On Mourning for the Dead

The following letter was written to a dear friend who was utterly broken down by excessive grief over the death of a beloved relative. I have suppressed the passages which were exclusively personal to the friend in question, but the letter as a whole might be addressed to any of those who mourn for their dead as those who have no hope.

At a Deathbed

I was often with you during the last illness of your dear one, and oh I did so want to help you, but I could not make you see me or hear. I was with you that day when she came over to our side. We were all waiting around for her, and I felt it would have been such a comfort to you to have told you just how happy she was with her mother and husband and the others. But, alas! Alas! You were all so unintelligent we could not make you hear anything.

A Tender Remonstrance

My own beloved, what do you mean by mourning as one who has no hope? Is it then all mere talk that Christ brought life and immortality to light? Why is it that with the certainty of the continued existence of your loved ones you feel as disconsolate and forlorn as if there were no other world, and as if Christ had never triumphed over death and the grave? Why by do you grieve as those who have no hope? Do you not know that you are as a city, set on a hill which cannot be hid? How many thousands, nay millions, of poor souls all over the world will have their lives saddened by the drip of your fears, who might have been gladdened by the sunlight of your smile – if you had only believed really in the love of God!

A Lost Opportunity

I do not say you have been very bad, I only mean to say that, whether from ill health or overstrain, you have not made the most of an opportunity. My dearest friend, I beg you not to think that I would dare to say these things to one to whom I owe so much, and from whom I learnt almost all that has been useful to me on this side, but I am on this side, and we can see things here which you cannot.

Joy the Natural Right of the Believer

I still hope you will be able to give to all the whole world an example, not of what is called Christian resignation, which is often only another word for despairing acquiescence, but the gladness and joy unspeakable that is the natural right of those who live in the love of God. This is not my message only. It is the message of all on this side. Why were you raised up, why are you set on high in order that all eyes may see you? I know you. Not for your own sake, but in order that you in your life may reflect His love to all who see you, as a mirror reflects the rays of the sun.

The Real Cause for Grief

My dear, dear friend, why do you not weep, not that your dear one is with us, but because you have made so little of the magnificent opportunity of proving to all that the other world is God's world to you, and that those who are lost to others are not lost to you who believe?

It is no use saying you believe if you don't believe. What is the use of saying you are warm if you shiver? I must beg of you not to be vexed with me, and not to think that I would say one word about anything that might grieve your mind, nor that we see so clearly, oh so clearly, what a chance there is now of proving to all the reality of Christ's triumph over death.

Conductors of God's Love to Man

What can I say to convince you? It is easy, you say, for me to scold you, but you cannot hear me, see me. You stretch out your hands in the darkness for your dear one who stands close to you, and you feel nothing, and you are disconsolate, and your heart rebels and you are unbelieving. Well, so far as you disbelieve, so far you lose your power to be the conductor of the love of God to man.

The secret of all power to help man is for you to be just the passive instrument in God's hands to teach, to show, to prove what he says. When self or unbelief comes in, there is weakness and loss of power. I don't mean by self what people call selfishness; I mean the darkness of material things which shuts us out from God and His Truth.

Grief a Measure of Unbelief

It is no use saying you believe when you feel sad. No one who really believes can ever feel sad. The measure of your grief is the measure of your unbelief. We who live in the atmosphere of the Love of God are often sad at our own imperfections. But where the deed is not ours but His, when the fact is what His wisdom and love have accomplished, not what our selfishness and sin have brought about, then all sorrow is the register of the spiritual thermometer of unbelief.

Death and the Sorrow of the World

Forgive me; I hate having to say these things to you, you who have been my teacher, to whom I owe all I am now, oh my own beloved friend. It is not pleasant for me to say these things. It is a hard thing. But I know your faith, and I know your love, and I trust to see them shine forth radiant and as the Love of God before the eyes of a sorrowing world. How awful a sight is the human race. Nothing you have ever said, or written, or dreamed could adequately express the sense of the horror of the sum of misery and anguish that prevails in the world by the presence of Death. By sin came death, Christ came to triumph over both. But He has not triumphed if those who call themselves by His name have no realizing sense of the immortality of their loved ones. Christ destroyed the dim veil that sin drew between the two worlds. Christ opened up the spirit world to those on earth.

The Work of Christ Partly Undone

But since His time that veil has been gradually restored, until now Death is as palpable a separation as it was in the pagan day. That is to be changed, and you are charged with one great part of the work of changing it. It is a proud privilege, a glorious opportunity. Go back, not as one who sorrows for the dead who are lost, but one who rejoices for the lost who are found. And if you are faithful, then will the joy of the Love of our Lord, which will fill your heart, be as the Dayspring from on high to the dim, sorrow-bleared eyes of the human race. Now, my dearest and honored friend, forgive me! What I write, I write not for myself alone, but for all on this side whose hope is placed in you. Goodbye.

Your loving friend, Julia.

The Law of Spiritual Growth

One of her communications, which came on the 18th June, 1893, was obviously addressed to me throughout.

Spirit Communication Not Harmful to the Spirits

I am over the border, but I am in constant communication with you on the earth-side. To me this has been the means of great blessing. I cannot conceive how anyone can consider that such communications can possibly retard growth. Growth depends upon love and service; and you limit the area of both when you put a wall of iron between the spheres. The conception of earth as a geographical place is very material. You think too much in matter. You cannot realize that to me and to all on this side you are spirit-fogged in a little body limited and conditioned by that fog. But the real self is spirit, not flesh-fog, and life is ministry and sacrifice and service and love. As, therefore, this means of communication enables me to minister to and serve those whom I loved, who are often sorely pressed and troubled, you can see how absurd is the doctrine that it is a hindrance to development.

The Lesson of the Incarnation

The question arises at once, Was Jesus wrong? Did His Incarnation impair or harm His Divine Nature. If not, then remember His own example. As He saved us, we also must save others, walking so far as we can in our Lord's steps. You are able to bear witness to the fact whether or not for the eleven months during which I have communicated with you I have ever sought anything but your welfare, and the welfare of your friends. Would it have been good for you to have been without my friendship? I have been ever near to you, and have more than once been able to tell you of what was to come, to explain what seemed mysterious, and generally to help and encourage you in all your work. What is there in this to harm one I am surprised that anyone should be so matter-minded as to imagine the earth-sphere is a geographical and not a spiritual limitation. No one is on the earth-sphere who lives in the spirit of the Lord. The place is immaterial; the spirit is everything.

The Wail of the Bereaved

Now, there are millions of good souls here whose love for those whom they left on earth is vast and consuming. There are mothers who have been taken away from their children; there are women who have lost their lovers and their husbands; there are numberless men who love and have lost their only joy in life when a gulf was made between them and those whom they loved. Oh, my dear friend, don't talk such nonsense! What is the use of saying they ought to find all consolation in the love of God? How is God revealed to me? He is revealed to them only when they love; there is no God where there is no love. Do you think that we, on this side, because we live more visibly in the presence of God, and are more consciously in the light of the love of our Lord, therefore love less those whom we loved on earth? I tell you, nay. It is quite the opposite. We love them more and more and more continually as we grow in grace and in the knowledge of the Lord.

The Barrier to be Broken Down

But how is it that we find ourselves thus cut off by a barrier from those whom we love?

Partly, no doubt, by our own fault. But, also, largely by yours.

One Army of the Living God

You have had teaching as to the communion of saints; you say and sing all manner of things as to the saints above and below being one army of the Living God, but when any one of us on the other side tries to make any practical effort to enable you to realize the oneness, and to make you feel that you are encompassed about by so great a cloud of witnesses, then there is an outcry. It is against the will of God! It is tampering with demons! It is conjuring up evil spirits!

Argumentum ad Hominem

Oh, my friend, my friend, be not deceived by these specious outcries! Am I a demon? Am I a familiar spirit? Am I doing what is contrary to the will of God when I constantly, constantly try to inspire you with more faith in Him, more love for Him and all His creatures, and, in short, try to bring you nearer and closer to God? You know I do all this. It is my joy and the law of my being. I should go on doing, it even if you were to refuse to let me use your hand. I am more privileged than most, because I can consciously interpret my action to you. But I am only doing consciously to you what is being done to others who are more or less unconscious of the influence they are subject to.

A Blessing from on High

Take my darling Ellen, for instance. I never write to her now with your hand, because I can, and do, constantly communicate with her direct. I do not visualize myself before her eyes; but she knows I am with her constantly, and always most with her when she is most troubled. But if you had not happened to be at F— , as you would say, Ellen would only have had a vague semi- consciousness, hardly daring to call itself a hope, that I was with her. Now she knows. And you can ask her whether the knowledge is not to her as a great blessing from on high.

The Ocean of Heavenly Love

Oh, my friend, my friend, you do not know the volume of refreshing water that will rush forth if you strike the rock, and save this people from perishing in the arid wilderness of unbelief. I am not now speaking about religion. I am speaking about love. There is love in this world like the water in the sea. Its waves are wailing and sobbing on the shore of human life; but you cannot bear, you do not understand. Why not try to flood your world with this heavenly love? Is it not worthwhile doing? If not, what is worth doing?

The Dangers of Communicating Across the Border

I want to say one word now about the danger of the communications about which you hear so much. I have not much to say. That there is love on this side is true. The devil and his angels are no mere metaphysical abstractions. There are evil ones, false ones, frivolous ones on this side, as there are on yours. You can never enlarge the scope and range of existence without at the same time enlarging the area of possible temptation and probable loss and peril. But the whole question is one of balance. And what I want to ask you is this: Do you or anyone else in your world ever cut off your communications with your children when they have gone into the larger life of a city, because they may bring you into the vortex of a city's temptations and the risk of evil and danger? You laugh at the suggestion. Why not laugh equally when those whom you love have passed on, not to New York, or Chicago, or London, but in the presence of God?

I do not ask that you should open a door into your souls through which all who feel disposed on this side should enter in to possess it. You can, if you like, either on this side or that, enter into companionship with the good or the bad. And I dare say that it is as true, on this side as on yours, that there is a possibility of making acquaintances who may be difficult to shake off. But so it is in London. You do not shrink from coming up to London from the country because in London there are many thousands of thieves, drunkards, swindlers, and men of evil and vicious life.

The Risk: Nothing to Love
You say you came up to London to do your work, and that it was therefore necessary to run the risk. Yes, and so it is necessary to run the risks of communicating with the wider field of spiritual existence. You say why? Oh, my friend, why? Is it necessary to ask that question, if so,

then you have never loved, or known the craving passion to help the loved ones? I rest the case on love. I will not argue it now upon what you believe and know, of the importance of realizing the segmentary nature of earth-life. I base it on the wide and universal want of the human heart not to have its consciousness of the presence and existence of the beloved suddenly severed by death – what you call death – which is really the entrance into life. It is necessary to risk the danger of evil spirits for the sake of keeping in conscious touch with the loved who have gone before.

Nothing Supernatural

And, believe me, the danger is monstrously exaggerated. It springs entirely from the false and foolish notions which have prevailed. If only you grasp the idea of the continuity of existence; if only you remember that, though the conditions of existence are altered, the life itself remains the same, you will no more have to face so many evils as those which come from believing that, when we speak to you, you are confronted by a kind of spiritual earthquake – a rushing into your life of something altogether supernatural. There is no such thing as supernatural. All is natural, and our Lord is the Lord of all.

SECOND SERIES – TO THE WRITER

1

After the Border Has Been Crossed

Although my communications with Julia have been more or less regular, for the last five years they been chiefly about matters in which I have been personally interested, and for nearly two years abstained from questioning her as to her life on the other side. In one of the last letters that she wrote, she excused herself from writing further at that time. She said she felt that it was almost a presumption for her to describe a country in which she had made so brief a, sojourn. Travelers should not attempt to describe a continent as soon as they land on its shores, and she adjourned for a season all communications on those subjects. This silence I respected, but at the close of 1894 Julia announced that she would resume her communications, and this is the result. The headings are my own. It will be noticed that here and there, in these communications, there are remarks by the way, asides, as it were, interrupting the tenor of the message. That is owing to questions that I ask, or mental observation that I make, as I read what my hand is writing. – W. T. S.

December 17, 1894

My Dearest Friend: – My duty to you and to those whom you reach is very grave. My task, however, is a pleasant one. For you are to allow me to tell those who are still in the body something more of the life which they will lead when their bodies are no longer useful.

In the Hour and Article of Death

In my earlier letters I told you how I experienced the change which you call Death. I have since then exchanged experiences with very many others on this side, and I now know more than I did then. With me the change was perfectly painless. I wish that it might be so always with all who are appointed to die. Unfortunately the moment of transition sometimes seem to be very full of pain and dread. With some it lasts a comparatively long time; I mean the time of quitting the body. With some it is momentary. The envelope opens, the letter is released, and it is over. Put sometimes the deathbirth is like childbirth, and the soul labors long to be free. There is no visible cause why this should be. That is to say, I do not know why some should pass so much more easily than others. That it is a fact is true. But, after all, the parting of soul and body is but an affair of moments. There is no reason to regard it with so much alarm. The tranquil soul that prepares and knows need not feel even a tremor of alarm. The preliminaries of decease are often painful; the actual severance, although sometimes accompanied by a sense of wrench, is of small account.

When the soul leaves the body it is at the first moment quite unclothed as at birth. The spirit-body disengaged from the physical body is conscious, at least I was, almost from the first.

I awoke standing by my dead body, thinking I was still alive and in my ordinary physical frame. It was only when I saw the corpse in the bed that I knew that something had happened. When the thought of nakedness crosses the spirit there comes the clothing which you need. The idea with us is creative. We think, and the thing is. I do not remember putting on any garments. There is just the sense of need, and the need is supplied. When we stand for the first time on this side there is not so much fear as great awe and curiosity. The sense of being in a land altogether undiscovered and unexplored, where there may be all manner of strange beings, perhaps hostile, fills you with a moment's trepidation. And then it is that the good Lord in His kindness sends to the newly delivered soul the Guardian Angel of whom I wrote before.

The Guardian Angel

So far as I have been able to ascertain, this Messenger of Love and Mercy meets all men when they die. In this there is no distinction made between the saved and the lost, and the Messenger is sent alike to all. But the lost have not the faculty to see him. The saved not only profit by his counsels, but feel him, and know he is with them. It is to all that the good Lord ministers – to all on your side and on this. His loving kindness is over all his creatures. But some know Him not, and when He would draw them nearer to His heart they are as if they saw, heard, felt nothing, But I think He loves best those who need Him most. The orphaned souls He cares for, though they see Him not; and they suffer, as it is necessary that they may be rid of the sin-stains which their loveless life has left upon their souls.

In Outer Darkness

The sinfulness of sin chiefly shows itself in the inability to see God. The punishment of sin which is remedial, is the sense of loneliness and darkness which overwhelms the loveless souls when they come into this world, the atmosphere of which is eternal love. This they endure until such time as they love. When they love they turn to God, and see in the darkness a ray of the Love infinite and everlasting, in which they are able to realize, as we do, that they live, and move and have their being.

There is much about this of which I will tell you later. For the present let me just say this: There is, when the loveless soul comes here, as much care taken to welcome it as when the soul of love arrives. But the selfish soul is blind and dark, and shudders in the dark. The imagination, which here is far more powerful than with you, fills the solitude with spectres, and the sinner feels he is encompassed by the constantly renewed visions of his deeds. Nor is this all; he sees those whom he has injured, and he fears. If ever a soul needs a Savior and, Deliverer, it is when imagination and memory without love recreate all anew the selfish acts of a loveless life.

Alone in a New World

December 18, 1894

When you stand all alone for the first time on this side there is not always, as you would think, a great longing to go back to the world you have quitted. The first sense is not that, but of awe, and of curiosity as to the new world. When I awoke I was so astonished and amazed at what I saw, and at the strangeness and sameness, I did not want to come back. The mind has not room for too many strong emotions at once. After the first shock of the entire novelty has subsided you begin to remember your friends. I remember seeing the nurse at my bedside and trying to speak to her, but I was soon convinced that it was impossible, and the new life lay before me.

You see it is this way: There is so much that is familiar and so much also that is unfamiliar, that you don't feel as if there was any immediate hurry to examine the old which you have seen all your life, and go on seeing, while there is so much that is new which you have never seen. You naturally are absorbed by the new, and only after you have felt and seen and understood what the new things are does your mind revert back to those whom you have left, and you wish to go back to tell them of what you have experienced.

No Desire to Return

Have you ever wished to be back again in this life? She wrote:

No, I have never for one passing moment wished to be back in my body again.

The body is such a miserable substitute for the spirit in which we live and move and act as we think. No, if I might come back and live on earth as I used to do, I would not; it would be all loss and no gain. There is nothing the body could give me, which I do not now enjoy. Only in an etherealized but more real way, and much that I enjoy I should lose by being again in my body.

No Separation From Friends

What about being parted from friends who survive?

That is, I admit, a deprivation to them and to you, inasmuch is you see them lamenting their deprivation. But it is not a real deprivation. You are with them to help them more than when you lived. When the departure entails material loss, as of the father who earns the money with which the family is supported, and the children are hungry, are scattered, or are sent to the poor house, you may think that it is hard to bear. And in one way it is. But you can have no idea of the abiding sense of the things which most impress us here. The first is the vivid realization of the love of God; the second is the exceedingly transitory nature of all earthly things; and the third, the extent to which poverty and misery minister to the creation of character, the development of love. These things make you feel very differently from what you, who are still immersed in the fever of matter, can quite understand.

The Difference of Perspective

We see so very differently the perspective. We realize that what often seems to you hard and cruel is the greatest benediction of the love of God. We know that He is Love, and what seems least loving is the irreducible minimum of suffering necessary to create the soul anew in the likeness of the love of God. Whatever else you may doubt, never lose hold of this: – God is Love. The atmosphere of the universe is the realizing sense of the love of God, and the more I live here the more impossible it seems to doubt it. The sun shines. The light of the sun fills the sky, and there is no doubt about it. God is Love. His love fills the universe; to us there is no doubt about it. Nor does the cloud or the night make us doubt the sun. And we do not doubt God because of the sin and the darkness where He is not seen. Oh, my friend! my friend! I am ashamed of the poor, paltry, miserable words and metaphors with which I am now trying to give you some idea of the abounding and overwhelming sense which we have of the love of God. That, my friend, is Heaven; and when you have it Heaven is there. All is summed up in that: God is Love, Love is God, and Heaven is the perfect realization of that.

December 28, 1894

What I want to write about this morning is the state of the disembodied soul immediately after death. When it meets the Guardian Angel there is usually a blank wonderment.

The Same Yet Not the Same
All is so new, and there are such unexpected samenesses as well as differences. When, for instance, we wake into the new life we are still in the same world. There are all the familiar things around us – the walls, the pictures, the window, the bed, and the only new things is your own body out of which you stand and wonder how it can be that it is there, and that it is no longer you. And then you begin clearly to understand what has happened. It is very much like experiences you have in dreams, which, after all, are often due to the same cause, the conscious soul leaving the physical frame, which, however, remains breathing. The first thing you notice that is not the same is the Angel. You are the same. I mean that there is no break in your consciousness, your memory, your sex I was woman in my bodily life, and I am woman still. There is no change there. But you are in a manner different.

On the Wings of Thought
The Angel Guardian who came to me had wings, as I

said. It is not usual, but if we please we can assume them. They are no more necessary than any of the contrivances by which you attempt to attain the mastery of the spirit over the burden of matter. We think and we are there. Why, then, wings? They are scenic illusions useful to convey the idea of superiority to earth-bound conditions, but we do not use them any more than we use steam engines. But I was glad my Guide had wings. It seemed more like what I thought it would be, and I was at once more at ease than I would otherwise have been.

The Voice of the Guide
When my Guide came he spoke to me in a very sweet, strong voice that had in it the confidence of the Invisible. And I was thrilled through and through with its note, which did not seem strange to me. Nor was this strange, for he had often been with me during my earth-life, although I had never seen him. I recognized him as an old and familiar part of myself, and this at first made me think that it was a woman. And when he said: "Come!" I did not hesitate. There was, as it were, a natural response to what seemed as the prompting of your own conscience. This is often the case. We have all our guides. These angels, unknown and unseen by us, prompt us to all good actions and dissuade us from evil. They are with us in thought, and we often receive their warnings as if they were the promptings of our own spirit. So they are; but the spirit which prompts is quite outside our own conscious self.

Our Higher Self
The Guardian Angel is indeed a kind of other self, a

higher, purer, and more developed section of your own personality. This is perhaps a little difficult to understand, but it is true. There are, as well as good, evil angels, who are with us no less constantly, and they are also sometimes visible as Angels of Darkness when we come across. They are with us always, and we are with them here when we leave our bodies. We are always swaying hither and thither towards our good and evil guides. We call them, or we did call them, impulses, wayward longings, aspirations, coming we know not where or whence. We see on this side where they come from.

The Senses as Blinkers

The soul in the body hears but dimly, and sees not at all the innumerable influences with which it is surrounded. The first and most startling thing we have to learn is that our senses, material senses, are not so much to help us to see and hear as to bar us off from seeing or hearing. We are on earth as it were, with blinkers on. We must not see or hear or know much that surrounds us. The physical consciousness which is part of us, needs for its development the temporary seclusion of life from the realities of the world of spirit into which it is ushered at death. Hence, when we close our eyes in the sleep of death, it is more of a laying down of the blinkers that limited and confined our vision than almost anything else. I am speaking of the conscious change to our senses.

God and Evil Spirits

We then can see what were the sources of these vague impressions, intuitions, and aspirations, both tip and down. We were in the midst of these Beings always, but we mistook them for parts of ourselves. They are distinct, although united, for no one can live to himself alone. We are all members one of another, and this is as true of spirits as of bodies.

These evil agencies exist. That I know. We see them; but we cannot fear them. For greater is He that is for us than all they that are against us. He is Love. And He is stronger than hate. The only power the Evil Ones have is due to our fear and lack of faith. They are powerless when we yield to the good Guardian who is ever near us, or when we know of God, who is love. I have not seen much of this evil side of life, and my information must be more or less second-hand.

A New Freedom of Movement
When I began to move I walked as I used to walk, and it seemed natural to do so. My Guide walked beside me, and we saw the world as it was with spirits moving among men. I did not see at first which was which. They were all living people it seemed to me. But I saw the spirits pass through matter and move away, as physical bodies could not do. Then I asked my Guide, and he said they were like myself, those who had lived on earth and had passed on. Then I saw that they moved sometimes as if they were still in the body, and at other times as if they were angels, coming and going with great speed, and I remarked upon it to my Guide. And he said, "Yes, they can do as they please, for it is in the power of the mind to go slow or fast."

Then I thought, if they can, I can. And I asked, not speaking, but thinking in my mind, if this were so? And my Guide, without my having spoken, answered and said, "This also is possible to you." And I said then to him, "May we go as they go whenever we are going?" And he smiled and said, "As you will, so it will be." And then I had my first experience of the new freedom of locomotion. The earth seemed to grow small beneath my feet.

A Flight Through Space

We went through space at a great speed. I did not feel the speed so much while in motion as when we stayed and discovered how fast and how far we had come. When we stayed it was not in this world at all. We had left your planet and were now speeding through space. I was hardly conscious of movement. We went as we think. Only the things we saw at first disappeared, and there was nothing to check or time our flight. We were together, my Guide and I. We went to a place at a great distance from your earth. The distance I cannot measure. Nor do we take account of distance, when you have only to think to be anywhere. The stars and the worlds, of which you see gleaming twinklings at night, are to us all as familiar as the village-home to a villager. We can go where we please, and we do please very often.

The Passion to Know

For there is one Passion that increases rather than diminishes on this side, and that is the desire to know and to learn. We have so much to learn and such facilities! We shall never be able to say we know everything about this world, for the marvellous wisdom of God is past finding out. When we reach what we think the ultimate, there is a new vista of marvels which we see before us.

We pass through, and when we come to a stand, beyond us again stretches a new invisible marvel-world, into which we also may at some new stage of development begin to see.

What oppresses us, if we may use the word, always and everywhere is the illimitableness of the universe. Up and down we see it unfolding always and ever. When we make the most effort to exhaust the subject the more inexhaustible it appears.

The Journey Beyond the Bounds

The journey which my Guide took me was a long one, how long I did not know. He led, I only willed to follow him. The motion was not flying. It was thought-transference of yourself. When I look back I see that it was made slower and simpler to give me the sense of distance. Now the movement is instantaneous. But then at first it was gradual. From walking we seemed to glide into the air without effort. The world simply sank away from us as when you are in a balloon; then it slid away behind, and we went through the air or through space in ether without landmarks. He went a little before me. I was at first a little frightened. But he was with me, and there was beside me such an exhilarating sense of liberty and power. You don't know what a prison the body is until you leave it. I exulted, I was so well, so free, so happy.

A Place Very Pleasant to Look Upon

(Question – What about those you have left in tears?)
No, I did not think much during the journey of those whom I had left behind. They were alive and well, and they would soon come over and be with me, the over

powering rush of new sensations seemed to leave no room for regrets or thoughts of the old life. Well, you may regret this, but I am telling you facts. You will find it so also your first day. And I think it is good and not evil. For otherwise it would have been different.

When we were journeying I spoke little. My thoughts were busy and yet I was not conscious of even thinking, only of feeling and seeing, drinking in at every point new impressions. When we seemed to be arriving at a new world, I spoke. I asked my guide, "Where is this? Is this Heaven?" He replied, "Wait and see. You will find those there who will teach you what you want to know."

The place was very pleasant to behold. The air was sweet, and there was a delicious fragrance as of flowers in June. The World – for it was a world we were approaching – seemed not unlike our old world, but it was different – there was nothing to jar. The sense of restful peace and contented love was everywhere. The place had a placid smile of tranquil joy; the note I remember, the details I will not enter upon.

2

Life on the Other Side

My Dearest Friend: – I wish to write with you quite a long letter this morning. I will postpone anything I may have to say about personal things, in order to tell you the message with which I am charged.

It is a message not personal to yourself, but general, and one which I wish you to publish in *Borderland*. We have not often so good an opportunity of addressing those who are still in their bodies, so I beg you to allow me the full use of your hand and pen for an hour at least.

Reunion With the Departed

You may remember that in my last I told you how we traveled to the land where I met my beloved friends. The meeting was very pleasant, but also in some way strange. There was a sense of difference. Those whom I met were still as loving as when I had bidden them adieu, but they were also somewhat different. There was nothing that reminded me of the pain and sorrow in which I had last seen them, they had grown spiritually. I felt myself a poor child beside them. Yet they were not haughty, only they knew more and loved more. They were very tender and kind to me. My Angel Guide handed me over to them. She said, "She needs what you can give her."

The first thing they were to teach me was to see those whom I knew on this side. That is almost always the way. I was no exception. When the soul wakes up on this side it is often encompassed about by those whom it has loved and served in life. But sometimes a little space intervenes, as was my case. Why, I shall tell you hereafter. But the space is small. We talk of space to you because you are still dominated by earth conditions, and when you come over here you find it difficult at first to escape from the old conceptions. They gradually fall off you as the chrysalis drops from the butterfly, but you will find that the Guide and the loving Father are wonderfully accommodating to your weakness and ignorance and prejudice.

Why They Did Not Meet

When I came here I had not lived long on earth. When I passed over I was still in the full energy of my prime. Among those who were here before were none who had been so close to me on earth as to make me long for them more than for all else. If Ellen, for example, had been on this side, my first thought would have been for her, and she would have been with the Angel. But as it was, all the longings of my heart were for those still on your side. My affections were set on the world and the souls still in the body. With regard to the New World, what I felt was more curiosity and wonder than the immediate passionate longing of the heart to meet those who had gone before. Hence the Angel met me alone. Hence the apparently long journey through space.

(Question – What about space?)

My dearest friend, it is impossible for me to answer all your questions. When you can understand what I might call the other side of everything, and can realize that the things seen are temporal, but the things unseen are eternal, you will be able better to understand what I am now trying to tell you as to the semblance of space.

Recognition

When I found my friends, there were about five or six of those relatives and near friends who had been on this side for some time. My dear little sister was the most loving and dearest of all. I saw before me the semblance of her childhood, just as she was in the long years ago, when I had parted with her it seemed forever. But she was only assuming the child-form to gain recognition. After a time, when I learned more about the life here, she revealed herself to me as we see her now, as a spirit who is a woman grown. There is no difficulty in our assuming whatever form we need for the purpose of the moment. No, I do not mean to say that I could assume permanently any disguise; but you can make yourself appear for the time what you think you wish to be. For the subtle thought is as an artist not merely in color or marble, but to all apparent semblance in the actual person.

The Analogy of the Double

You should not marvel at this, for have you not many proofs of this even on your side in the phenomenon of the Double? Yes, the Double only reproduces himself. But if you, when you are still encumbered with bodies of flesh and blood, can reproduce your apparently real and living counterparts, clothed sometimes in dresses which exist only in your thought, why should you doubt that we can do the same, only to a much greater extent? We have no need to do so for our own purpose; but when a new comer arrives, or when we have to manifest ourselves to you who are still in the body, then we need to use this thought-creation, and body forth the visual tangible appearance with which you are familiar.

(Question – Can you tell me how to do this?)

No, I will not enter upon that subject, there is much more important matter to write about than these induced materializations.

The Chief Surprise

My little sister having embraced me, and welcomed me to the sphere where the loved and the lost are united, took me by the hand and brought me to the friends who were close by waiting for me. They were all very kind and loving, and they told me many things. The chief surprise that I found was in the fact that we were all so very much the same. We did not seem to have become angels or saints. For my part I was, I fear, by no means saintly. There was at first a certain awe that numbed me; but as that numbing sensation wore off, my old natural self asserted itself, and I really felt that I was as I had been, only with a much greater sense of power and of freedom. There was the increased sense of vitality – doubly and trebly delightful after my illness – and a great feeling of restful absence of fret.

No Sense of Perfection

But don't imagine that I felt myself a saint or in angel; I did not, and I fear that I do not now. The sense of imperfection is still with us. Oh, my friend, my friend, there are heights to scale which you have not dreamed of; there are depths of infinite love which we have not even attempted to fathom. Arid the more we see, and know, and understand of the Divine love, the more we feel lost in the contrast between the immensity of His love and the infinitesimal meagerness of our own souls. But the difference between what we feel here and on earth is that here the consciousness of love is everywhere. We see what we are, and we often regret it, and mourn for our shortcomings. But we know that we live in the very love of God, and that our very stumblings tend upwards. But we do stumble and fall short of the glory of God.

The Persistence of Individuality

Even here! Oh, my friend, my friend, do you think that if that bundle of passionate and eager forces which make up what you call your Ego were to come here, if the earthly house of your tabernacle were to be dissolved, that you would, in a moment, in a twinkling of an eye, be quite other than you are? Would that spirit of yours be freed from the characteristics which make you really you? No, I tell you no. Individuality is not eliminated, but rather accentuated in its essence, and harmonized in its accidents. The trouble in the world is that there it is the other way. There is so much friction in the horns and hoofs and armor of individuality that the real individuality often perishes.

No, I don't mean that we never get into a temper; but we are in what you might call a moral and spiritual sanitarium. We have brought with us all our diseases. We get cured. You can understand that by analogy with the effect of certain climates on earth on physical maladies. The ozone of our life here is love. And, my dear friend, if you had but love enough you would have heaven where you are. Believe me, that there is no truth greater than this. God is Love! God is Love!

How Love Makes Heaven

And heaven differs from earth most of all in this. There is more love in it; and every love that throbs in the human heart makes earth more like heaven. No, I will not be led into a discussion about different loves. I have written about that before. All that I need say now is that the love which takes you out of yourself, and makes the happiness of another so important to you as to make even pain and trouble joyous, and more to be desired than the greatest pleasures, if they are for the welfare of the beloved, that love is the love that overcomes the world. Sin is only the absence of love. Sorrow would be turned into joy if only you loved. I know what you mean. But the sorrow that comes from loving one too much – no, you can never love any one too much. You often love others too little, and the misery you feel because, as you say, you love one too much, is really because you love the other too little.

And Lack of Love Hell

You have, for instance, lost, by parting or by misunderstanding, some one whom you idolize. You are wretched, and life seems dark, and there is no object worth living for. This darkness and misery are not because you love, but because you don't love. For that which troubles you is the void, the blank left in your life. You have never mastered the secret of the true life until you have learned that love is the magic wand that can transform the world, and that wherever it is not transformed it is because you do not love. For instance, if your heart was always full of love for all men as it is for the woman whom you most passionately adore – if every human or sentient being were so much loved by you that you were as much rapt into ecstasy by a chance of helping them, and of making them glad, as you are by similar opportunities for her whom you love – you would never be a blank, nor existence a burden. No, my dearest friend, believe me when I say, whatever else I may have to teach you, there is nothing that for a moment is comparable in importance to this – the open secret of heaven's love. He who dwells in perfect love is in heaven. Hatred is hell, and God is with all who love. God is love. Those who do not love are without God.

Death Exists – for the Living

But your questions and objections take me away from what I was saying. When I came to talk with my friends; they told me many things that at first startled me. They said, for instance, that I should be able to go among all those whom I had left, and that I should feel no sense of separation. For the spirits of our friends are open to us on this side. Then I said, "There is no death," and they laughed merrily. "Of course not," they said, "not to us who are 'dead.' Death is only a sense of deprivation and separation which the so-called living feel – an incident of limitation of 'life.' Death only exists for the 'living,' not for us." And I wished at once to go and see if it were so; and immediately as I thought, I was back among those whom I loved. I saw Minerva, and tried to make her see me. I saw Ellen, and she would not listen to me; and so I came back and said: "No, there is death." They cannot hear, or see, or speak, or feel my touch. And my friends said, "There is death for the body, and those who are in the body feel death even when in life; but when they sleep, and some when they wake, they can hold converse with the spirit before death." And, as you know, I have found it so. But sometimes the soul is so immersed in matter; it is so preoccupied with the affairs of the world, that even when sleep liberates the higher soul it sees nothing of us. Mostly, however, we can see, and speak, and communicate freely with the spirits of our living friends. But they seldom can communicate their impressions to the physical consciousness, which is to us almost as inert and unimpressionable as the body of a man asleep is to the living men around.

The Meeting With Jesus

March 22, 1895

My Dearest Friend: – May I resume my message? Thanks, so much. When I had tried in vain to communicate with Minerva and with, Ellen, I began to be a little sad. It seemed to me as if I were away from the real interests which bound me to life. It was, no doubt, very pleasant to be well, and delightful to move about as freely as you think; but stilt the people I loved most, and the work I was most wrapped up in, were there; and I was rather sad. Then it was that the Good Angel who had welcomed me into this world took me to see my Lord. I have nothing to add to what I wrote before.

Sadness and Sorrow Fled Away

It was beautiful and glorious, exceeding all my powers

of description. There was no expectation of the meeting, nor was I even able to realize the fact that I had met Him until I saw the whole landscape flame and glow as with the radiance of opened heaven when He spoke to me. The cause for this difficulty was, I suppose, the extreme naturalness of all that I saw and heard. There is such a difficulty in realizing that today, as yesterday, is the same. When there is something of what we used to call the supernatural order coming in the midst of what seems so very natural, it is difficult to realize it. But, oh, my friend, when it is realized, what a change occurs! The whole world was transfigured in the realization of the intensity and constancy of His love. And from that moment I have never been sad, save for my own shortcomings and my own lack of love. Oh, my dearest friend, if only we could live more in the realized sense of His love.

(What about the Divinity of our Lord?)

The Divinity of Jesus

Oh, why do you trouble yourselves about these scholasticisms? The thing that matters to you is surely what is – not what may have been defined centuries since. My dearest friend, when you come to this side and have a more vivid sense of the majesty and marvel of the universe; when you see, as we do every day, the great unfolding of the infinite glory of the Infinite Father; and when you see also, as we do, that the whole secret of all things is Love, and that there was never so much Love revealed to mankind as in Him, you can understand how it is true that there dwelt in Him the fullness of the Godhead bodily.

March 23, 1895

My Dearest Friend: – That is right, be quite passive; ask no questions, but allow me to write as if I were using my own hand. What I want to say to you, and, through you, to the world of men and women among whom I once lived as an embodied spirit, is not a message which you can help out by eager questionings. Ask me what you please after I have done; but, meanwhile, make your mind as passive as possible, I will do the writing.

The Divine Power of Love

Now, my dear friend, I wish to go on from where I left off, telling you, as far as I can, consecutively what my experiences were when I first found myself here.

"When my spirit awoke to consciousness of the eternal life and its surroundings, I found myself in company with bright and blessed angels, the ministers to me of the abounding mercy of God. The shock that severed me from earth had been so sudden that at first I was not conscious that I was in the spirit world. But my dear father made himself known, and convinced me that I was indeed alive and amongst the ranks of the shining ones. With him was my dear mother; and they were joined after by the pure spirit of Keble, and philanthropic souls who delight to gather around him who on earth was a chief amongst men in philanthropy and deeds of love. By them I was conducted to the home where my guardians rest. From them I learn that which is requisite for me, and am taught to put aside much that I once thought of vital moment. Ah! How easily does the spirit put away the opinions of earth to which it so fondly clung! Through my guardians I received the request that I would put myself into communication with you. It was conveyed to me through your presiding spirit, who now writes for me. I complied with joy, and am now pleased beyond measure that I can touch the plain where so many dear to me still live; though alas! alas! I cannot reach them. They know not, and will not learn as yet. Since I left the earth I have been occupied in learning my work, and in preparing myself for the life of progress to which my being is now devoted. Already, under the guidance of my guardians, I have passed through the first sphere, where are gathered those who are bound to earth by the affections, or are unable to rise as yet. There I saw some whom I ha had known in the body, and learned from them, and from others, much that I needed to know. My work will be of a similar sort till I reach my appointed sphere. I have come to give you this brief word of comfort and consolation. Be of good cheer."

"One has so much to ask. Are the spheres like this world?"

"In every way similar. It is only the change of conditions that makes the difference. Flowers, and fruits, and pleasant landscapes, and animals, and birds, are with us as with you. Only the material conditions are changed. We do not crave for food as you; nor do we kill to live. Matter, in your sense, is done with; and we have no need of sustenance, save that which we can draw in with the air we breathe. Nor are we impeded in our movements by matter, as you are. We move freely, and by volition. I learn by degrees, and as a new-born babe, to accustom myself to the new conditions of my being."

"Are things real to you?"

"Quite; and very beautiful" on this side. When I had seen the splendor of the love-light that flooded the world, I was beside myself with joy. All the many loves which I had known on your side faded into insignificance beside the great glowing radiance of that love which swathed me about as with a garment and enabled me to see what marvellous possibilities, what undreamed-of powers were all the while in the heart of each of us. For there is no other word for it but love. God is Love, and Love is God, and the mystic power of God is Love. We may become as God so far as we enter into His divine nature, which is love. We may be God as we love, and we remove ourselves from God as we don't love. When you feel as if you were unable to sympathize with any person, by so much as you are unable to sympathize even with his sins, you are out of God. He is all in all, and all His all is Love; and you cannot work out His purposes in hate and unkindness. Oh, if only I could make you see as we see it here, how true it is that they only live who love; that all that is not love is as death; that the soul that does not love is without God in outer darkness; and the only way to save the world is to drench it with love; yes, love even for the worst. It is not by disliking men, even for their sins, that you will save them from their sins. Pardon me, but this is the truth; all else that I can tell you is but as the fringe; this is the central essence of all.

The Impression Left by Jesus

When I had, as it were, recovered from the delighted amazement of the new light, I felt overpowered by a sense of the marvellous condescension of my Lord: for there was about Him nothing, of the majesty that terrifies and

72

repels. The one supreme idea, which He left on my mind, was that of the infinite attraction of love; and a love, too, that was personal to myself. There was no jealousy in my love, but I felt that He loved me as much personally as He loved any one; and He wished for my love, and that without it neither he nor I could be complete. (I know you think this is a blasphemy; I should have thought so once.) But there is the incompleteness of the not yet re-alized ideal; and the thought of God will not be com-pletely embodied until every heart throbs in responsive love without one jarring note to the All Lover, in whom we live and move, and have our being.

And with the great new joy in my heart I talked with Him.

What I meant and what He understood was very simple. I longed, simply longed, with an all-constrain-ing desire to make known this love that passeth all un-derstanding to those I loved; and He smiled with loving satisfaction at me as I spoke, and I knew that I was not denied.

The Patience of God
But I was not then allowed to begin my work. What I had to do was the beginning of preparation for my work. I had to learn so much; and among the lessons I had to learn, this above all was enforced upon me, to apprehend the patience that waits. He waits; for with Him time is not, and He sees the end from the beginning. And when we, in our impulsive eagerness, would rush in and change, forgetting that time is but a mode of thought, He re-strains us; and I was restrained. But it seemed hard; I wanted to go at once and tell you what the truth of the

world is. But I must wait. Wait and learn. And I was prepared to execute my mission.

March 31, 1895

My Dearest Friend: – I gladly continue my message. You
are so busy; I sometimes fear that I shall never be able to
tell you what you want to know.

Character the Only Test

The worth of character, which you sometimes ignore
and never rightly recognize, must be seen as we see it
here to be appreciated. We have wonderful surprises
here. We see men as they are. Not, of course, all men always. But when the wrappings are off, we see the nature
of the soul, and the factor that decides is the character.
I know this sounds like a commonplace. But it does not
seem a commonplace when it is applied as we see it applied here. No. You can hardly, by any stretch of imagination, realize what a change it is to live in a place where
the only test is character, where property, station, and
work do not count – no, nor religious profession. The
idea that you so often have in the world, that the words
which you say with your lips have magic influence on
your hearts, must be seen in all its hollow absurdity to
be understood.

Judge Not

We see things as they are, not as they are labeled. We
have such surprises to encounter; such amazing upturns
and revolutions of the estimate in which Men and wom-
en are held. Oh, my friend, my friend, if the first word
of my message is, God is Love, and those who Love are

living in God, my second word surely must be: Judge not. Judge not. For you cannot see, you cannot understand. You are all as children in the dark making guesses at the colors of shadows thrown upon a screen. You do not see, the color, and yet you pronounce confident judgment. Judge not until at least you see the man as he is. Often what seem to you the worst things are the best. Sometimes the apparent best are among the worst. Motive is not everything, but it is a great deal – so much that those from whom motive is hidden cannot judge fully. My own experience of all this was very varied, and I soon became accustomed to disregard all the distinctions I had made so much of when in life. Then I used to ask if So-and-so were religious, whether he belonged to this or that or the other church; now these things do not interest me any more than the new frills and facings of fashion. We don't ask what church. Here let me say that you may misunderstand what I have written. It is not that I think being religious is of no importance. It is of all importance.

Churches and Real Religion
What I meant was the asking of any one of his church connection as a way of knowing whether or not he was religious. That is the absurdity we never practise. We never ask about these things except so far as they stand in the way of the real religion. We lament, and have continually to deplore, the fact that they are substituted for the love which is the fulfilling of the law. The degree of love with which any one loves, measures his religion.

The Test of Irreligion
The degree of hatred, or indifference which paralyzes

love in the soul, is the test of irreligion. Love eats into selfishness as the sun's rays eat into the black and dark night. That is God in life. That is what we see. Light that shines in the darkness. Love is that light. We don't care for the shape of the shutters that shut it out. Nor for the endless discussions, as to the windows that let it in. These questions are so simply answered.

The Best Test of a Church

The best window, what is that? It is the window that lets in most light. Where, then, is the light that is the test of the window? And the light of life is Love, and Love is God and God is Love; and those who do not love are those who sit in outer darkness, and in the valley of the shadow of death. Sin consists in the living without God; that is to say, without love. But the more you think the more you see that love that is selfish is not love, and love that injures its object is not love but cruelty. The love that sacrifices the permanent welfare of the loved one, to the immediate gratification of the pleasure of the moment, is not real love. All love supposes some degree of restraint, and this is true of the Highest as well as of men and women. Restraint that is born of the intelligence that foresees. And real love is the keenest-sighted of all things.

3

How to Widen the Chinks

September 18, 1896

I have much to say to you, and I hope that you will be quite passive and not interrupt me.

Charged With a Message
Now listen. I am going to write a letter to the readers of *Borderland,* which will be a very useful communication. We have been thinking it over for a long time, and I am charged to deliver it to you at the first opportunity. I will write it straight away, and continue day after day till it is finished. I think it will take me about a week to finish it. And you must let me have the uninterrupted use of your hand. It is to give them what we know to be the most important advice that there is to give for the conduct of life.

The Thought of God
We have all seen with intense interest the efforts which man is making at present to discover, if he can, what lies beyond. We who are beyond are not less anxious to communicate to you – who have still to slough your bodies – what will be the best for you on earth to know, in view of the new life which awaits you. And I had hoped that, in the letters which I began in *Borderland,* to have explained many things. But they were interrupted, and I now see that it was better so.

No Claim to Infallibility

We who have ceased to dwell in matter often make mistakes in our expectations, as you do, and err in our judgment. No one save Him who is above all knows all. We are not made infallible because we put off our bodies. We see many things you do not. But we are making progress through darkness into light, through ignorance into knowledge. And hence it is that while we may, and I hope often will, say what will help you and enable you to guide your way better, we never arrogate to ourselves the right to dictate. We are only too glad to impress you with our thought. But it is not Divine wisdom – only the thought of your friends who, being disencumbered of their earthly bodies, have the open vision, and dwell in the land of Love and Light.

Not New Light But More Light

Our chief difficulty in framing our message is the fact that we have nothing to say that has not been anticipated, more or less, by one or other of those messengers who have taught men the way to God. But this is obvious. You have to recognize the fact that God has not left you in darkness all these ages, nor has he given you misleading light. What we have to do is not to give you what I may call a revolutionary revelation, so much as to widen the chinks through which the same light may stream through a little more clearly. The fullness of the glory of that light we cannot describe. We who dwell in it are discovering more and more of the imperfection of our vision. And so it will ever be. Progress, eternal progress, ever forgetting the things that are behind, ever reaching forward to those which are before it, is the universal law.

There are many things, however, on which we think it possible to widen the chinks. And I will at once proceed to explain what it is that we wish to impress upon you as most important.

(Remark – I thought at once, "Love?")

The Gospel That Will Save the World

I am not going to repeat what I have often said before about Love. There is nothing to add to or to take away from what I said about love when I first wrote with your hand.

Where God Is

For the identification of love, wherever it is found as God, as a ray from God, pure and bright, the authentic emanation from God, in proportion as it is unselfish and sacrificial in its nature, that is the Gospel which will save the world. And when men ask you where God is, then you can answer, where Love is. That I have said before, and I might go on saying it always. But repetition would not widen the chinks.

And what we want to do is to widen the chinks, through which more of the light and glory of this world may stream into the world in which you live.

A Reproof

Yes, it can be done if you will but be passive and not make your mind a whirling wheel of interrogation. When you are done asking, I may get on writing. But when your mind is so excitable and runs along so many of its own channels, I cannot trust your hand as the instrument whereby to transmit my message.

Yes, I can understand. But the understanding why does not suffice to make the instrument work. When you are passive I shall resume my message. It is of great importance to have a passive, quiet, receptive mind.

September 19, 1896

Now to resume where I left off.

Her Message

What we wish most to say to you is that you should endeavor to resume the habit of contemplation. You are all too much hurried. You are all getting to be too busy. How do you think that you are to keep the door open between you and Him who is Love, unless you have at least some moments in the day when you can be alone with Him, and with us? Oh, my friend, when we see you absorbed day by day, and far into the night over the things of your life, being so preoccupied that no voice from the other side can reach your ears, what chance have you to grow in the knowledge of the Spirit? About as much as a girl dusting out a boarding house in a hurry has of learning the higher mathematics Oh, my friend, what the world needs is an arrest of this fretful fever about trivial things, which perish with the using.

What the Age Most Needs

What the age needs is time to think, time to meditate, time to pray, time, in short, for the Divine and Eternal. What is it that we most need in our efforts to bring this world of ours into touch with yours?

Why have I failed with you, comparatively? Why is the Bureau I wrote about years ago not established? All because of one thing, and one thing only. You have no time. That is to say, that all the time you have, you spend on the things of this whirling transitory life. It will not do. Your world will gain no glimpse of the other side, open we the chinks never so widely, when the whole day is spent in the desperate pursuit of an unceasing multitude of this world's affairs. No; to truly live, you must make time to think; to clear, for some moments at least, a silence where our voices may be heard. That is nothing new, but the world seems to be forgetting it more than of old. We can do nothing to establish the connection unless, for at least some brief season, you can say to yourself;

"Peace; be still!"

Five Minutes' Meditation
We do not ask impossibilities. We do not wish men in a newspaper office to practice the contemplative life of the monks of the Thebaid. But we do affairs possess them. But if there were but five minutes in every day in which to possess their souls in peace. All the rest of the day the world and its affairs possess them. But if there were but five minutes daily for the soul for quiet thinking on the relations between you and love – which is God manifest in life – would it not be better for you? Would you not have more chance of the open vision that you have lost?

(Question – Am I not myself suggesting the illustrations at least!)

An Explanation by the Way
Oh, my friend, bow little you understand the working of Mind on mind. All that I see in your mind – knowledge

of the English language, for instance, or associated ideas – are to me so much material by which I can get my thought into your consciousness. All your stored-up ideas, memories, associations, are like the letters inside a typewriter. I strike whatever I need. The alphabet was yours, but the touch was mine.

What is necessary to be done is to get the idea impressed on the mind of this generation, Rest. And whatever there is in your mind that I can use to impress this idea I use without hesitation. It is easier working with familiar tools. When I try to make you write words with which you are not familiar I fail, at least as often as I succeed. Hence, I am always more pleased when I can revive an old idea, or use a metaphor that would be familiar to you, than if I were to laboriously try to move your fingers to trace words which you had never seen before.

Now I hope you understand. What I want you to say I make you feel in the readiest way possible, always your own language and your own ideas as use your own pen and your own handwriting. But I use them to impress my idea, to deliver my message.

Don't Crowd God Out of Your Life

And what we have to say to you and through you first of all is this: You must have time to think of God and of His Manifestation as Love, otherwise you will crowd God out of your life; and a life without Love, is a life without God. What you all need is a halting-place now and then; a resting-place in which the angels of God can commune with the soul. What chance have you of realizing the truths of the other world if you are perpetually racing to catch trains in this? I know you must catch trains, but what I plead for is that you should make time, at least for a few minutes a day, in which to catch Eternity or a glimpse of it and of Eternal things.

Yes, that will do. I will write tomorrow.

September 27, 1896

Now then to resume. It is a mistake to say that there is no longer time in which to think. With the increased rush there are many oases. But with the continued rush there disappears the capacity to utilize them. And what I wish to do today is to point out some of the methods in which the lost Meditation-time may be recovered.

Meditation Times
What I want meditation-time for is to get a chance at your soul. The mundane and material veil the soul from us. We catch fitful glimpses of your soul as if through thick hanging clouds. We want to see more of it. And to influence you more in Time with the thought of Eternity.

To do this we must get you to help. And the first way to help is to teach you how to utilize your spare moments. Here let me answer that thought of yours as to the idleness of purposeless meditation. It is not my purpose that your meditation should be purposeless.

To Develop Love
What I want you to do, if you find an opportunity, is to modernize the Rosary. What you have to do is to get the ordinary man who will not pray, and who is not given to spiritual meditation, to take the first steps towards the realization of the Divine. This you can do only in

83

one way. Where Love is, God is. There is no formula so true as that. To get man into the presence of God, make him love. And the worst sign of the latter times is when the love of many has grown cold. But do not quench the smoking flax Break not the bruised reed. Wherever life is, love is not impossible. For the complete absence of love is the final cessation of life. Love is often latent as heat is. But the development, the expansion of love – that is the growth of life.

First, for Your Higher Self

Hence the use of the meditation-moment is primarily the development of Love. And this can be done quite simply by giving the Divine nature within each a free chance to assert itself. For all around man lies the quickening Spirit of God. And you have but to allow it a chance instead of hustling it out of the way to see the God-germ grow.

(Question – Must man, then, think first of self and not of the others?)

Now you are surprised and I see your thought. But what a man ought first to think of when he meditates is himself. What am I making of myself? For love begins at home. And if a man is cruel to his own soul – ? No, you must care for your higher self, the God within. What are you doing with that? Giving it exercise? And what? Since when has it had an opportunity of doing anything worth doing? And are you stunting or starving or killing it? Soul-murder – are you guilty of it? For it is possible to murder your own soul.

Second, for Your Enemies

And then the next thought must be, my enemies, what

good have I done them? For an enemy is the man with whom you have failed. It may not be your fault, but if he is your enemy, you have failed; for it is failure when any fail to realize that one is your Father, and all ye are brethren. Whom you dislike, that is an enemy – a failure. Have you done anything to make him a success? You may do nothing. But have you thought kindly of him, pitying his blindness, and big shortcomings, longing to see him better?

(Question – But sometimes it is best kindness to punish?)

Yes, I know you are quite right in thinking that there are times when it is necessary to punish evildoers; but as you punish, love! And remember that punishment without love is not of God. Have, then, a list, long or short, of the people you dislike, and run over them lovingly. Out of joint with this, with that, with the other-this is not in the Divine order, and you ought to try to be in charity with, that is to like, all men.

Thirdly, for Your Friends

Then your friends and those to whom you are related. Your success depends upon individualizing. Take each in turn. What have you done for him, for her, since yesterday? What have you left undone?

In short, evil is the want of thought. Think – a loving thought is a prayer. You have not time to pray? Then make time to think of those you love. Without thinking on to people you lose vital connection with them. To all men and women you know you owe some duty, however slight. It may be a smile, it may be a word, it may be a letter, it may be praise, it may be blame; and there is more love needed to blame rightly than to praise. But whatever it is, it is due from you to each of these. Have you paid your dues? Not in the lump, but to each his due?

What is the excuse for half the unkindness in the world? What is the cause of most of the sadness? Not poverty of this world's wealth, but poverty of loving thought. You do not think; you forget. You neglect for want of thought. You allow the love that is in you to grow cold. For love dies when you never think of the person loved.

Thought as Prayer

Therefore think of them all. If you can do nothing else, think of them lovingly for the loving thought of a friend is an angel of God sent to carry a benediction to the soul.

Yet, in this way we all fulfill, or help to fulfill, our own prayers. You see dimly in your gropings in the region of telepathy the influence of thought, and you will discover more, much more, ere long. But when you think with real feeling and earnestness of another's welfare and long to help him, you do help him. Here is, as it were, the secret source whereby the fire is fed which would else have flickered out and died. Oh, my dearest friend, if you only knew the power of thought, and if you would but think, think, think!

Now I have ended for today. Tomorrow I will open up the second point of my message. But do not forget my first. The supreme need of the soul of man is time to think, which means time to love, i.e., time to live.

The Bureau of Communication

September 26, 1896

All that is written has been well written. Nor do you need to disturb yourself about whether it all comes from me or from your Subconscious Self. When you know all about your Subconscious Self, as you call it, you will understand. What is important is that, however directed, you should get my message right. The first word of my message was Love, the second Leisure, and now we come to the third and what you may deem the most practical part of my message. I mean the old and very important application which I made to you about the Bureau of Intercommunication between the Two Worlds.

A Remonstrance

I have never for a moment ceased longing for its establishment. There is something to me almost inconceivably pathetic in the yearning that all of us here have to be able to communicate with you on your side. And what saddens me so much is that while I see so clearly how it, can be done, you do riot as you ought try and help me to do it. What a long time there has been since I first came to you. And what have you done? What progress has there been made towards this indispensable Bureau? My friend, my friend, why have you tarried so long? Why, when the Borderland is mournful with the sighs of the severed, have you done so little to unite?

(Remarks. – Excuses, various, suggested in reply to this reproach: (1) Preoccupation; (2) difficulty of finding available trustworthy mediums: (3) difficulties in the way – (a) personation, (b) elementals, (c) evil spirits; (4)

disappointments and failures. When I have tried you have not been able to manifest to some clairvoyants, and have never been able to be photographed. Health, also, this last year, etc.)

Excuses Brushed on One Side

Yes I know all that. But what does it all come to? Nothing at all. Nothing at all. Any one who allowed himself to be deterred by such excuses would never achieve anything. Now what I want you to brace yourself up to is to answer this question – Is the establishment of an assured and verifiable mode of communication between us and you an object worth trying for? Is it not the one thing of all other objects best worth trying for? What other object is so important as to prove beyond all doubt that all that the saints and sages have taught is true, that when the body is put off the spirit lives, that when men "die" they begin a new life which is not cut off by any impassable abyss from yours? And what I want you to do is to put this question fairly and squarely to your conscience. And then, having answered it, act. Do not say, "Yes, it is the most important thing," and then subordinate it to the most trivial. Don't say, "Yes, I think this is the supreme thing, mankind needs," and their leave the quest to chance or caprice. All that is not rational.

Is It Worthwhile?

(Remarks. – Yes; I agree if the chance of achieving were good enough to justify the needful sacrifice of time and energy. But I have seen so many so utterly disappointed after years of patient investigation that I, who am busy with pressing duties, feel the chance is small indeed of my

succeeding where they have failed.)

How do you know that they have failed? What you have to do, surely, is to see whether your own chance, as you call it, is worthwhile. And what I tell *(Remarks. – Interrupted. Resuming, two hours later, I observed, that this is the kind of thing that always happens.)*

An Exhortation

What I tell you is that you ought to take the subject more seriously. You are dealing with the highest of things as if it were a mere holiday pastime, to be put on one side whenever any obstacle has to be overcome. Now if, as I know you believe that this is the most important thing that lies before mankind, will you begin to apply yourself seriously to the matter?

(Question – What do you mean by seriously?)

By seriously I only mean that you should prosecute the study with the same serious resolution and business-like methods that you devote to the study of much less important things. You see there is no chance of doing anything from this side unless you will help. Give me your time, and I will give you my assistance.

(Question – How much time?)

Half an Hour a Day

My dear friend, why do you speak so grudgingly? You know how ready I have always been to make allowance for your work. I do not want you to give up any of your work. That is your first duty. But I think that if you tried, really tried, you might get half an hour always before starting, work. That is what I ask – that for half an hour always before breakfast you allow me the use of your hand in order that I may make some sustained systematic effort to accustom you to the method of intercourse with us on this side. When you are dead tired I will not press you. But, as a rule, let me have the opportunity.

(Question – I wonder if it will be any good?)

You are a doubting Thomas. Yes, it will be of good. Great good, as you will very soon perceive. Yes, I know that there have been mistakes – yes, and there will be. Your own experience with the phonograph should illustrate how difficult it is to read off the transcript. But courage! As for the mistakes you think of, they are not mistakes except as to time, and we sometimes fail to distinguish thoughts from things. But it is only by experimenting, patient, loving experimenting, that we, you and I, can learn how to avoid these errors. Now, my friend, good-by. If you will begin at once, I will do what I can to realize the longing of the heart of man.

$$4$$

The Use and Abuse of Spirit Communications

The Proposed Bridge Across Borderland

December 5, 1906

My Dearest Friend: – I am now going to give you what we think on this side is a word of advice which is much needed. You are very eager to make a Bridge, you say, between the two worlds. And we are more so. But when you say this, do you realize what it implies? What the realization would effect? I am more and more convinced that the establishment of the fact, and the certainty of communication between this world and yours, may be described without exaggeration as the most important thing in the whole range of the possible achievements of mortal man. There is nothing like it for the far-reaching influence which it will exercise over all things. For it will modify thought, and thought makes the world in which you live. No one can understand how true that is when he is still immersed in matter.

Its Effect on the Focus of Life

You must not, therefore, think that I am drawing back or wish in the least to deter you from the task to which you have set your hand. But before you seriously begin to bridge the gulf, I think that it would be only right to point out to you what it will do, or rather what it will bring about. For it will alter the focus of life.

The focus of life is at present, to the majority of men, confined between birth and death. The focus will be changed when once you make it clear, not as a may be, but as a scientific certitude, that we live here and can communicate with you. And when you alter the focus of life, what is it that you do? You alter the perspective of everything.

A Change Not Altogether Good

You cannot realize how changed a world it will be. The change will, I know well, be for good and mainly for good. But no revolution ever was which did not do, incidentally, much evil, and your bridge will not be any more than anything else, an unmixed benefit. You must be prepared for many disappointments, and you will often wish you had never touched the subject. The work of the bridge-builder is to cross the abyss. And abysses are abysses. They are not paradises. And the more useful the work the more it will be opposed. No, don't imagine that it is easy. Via Dolorosa, always Via Dolorosa – the dolorous way is the Via Crucis. But it is the way of salvation.

Well, then, I will go on. First, you will alter the focus of life. That you see. The perspective, which is right when the focus is fixed by a limited line, becomes wrong when the line is drawn out indefinitely. You are impatient. But I will go on.

How It Will Affect the Churches

Secondly, you will, in so far as you are successful, destroy as by a sudden – [here I was interrupted]. Where have I left you? No, it is nothing; you were rung off. Oh, yes, I was saying that you will destroy, as if by a sword-cut or razor-slash, the whole theory of the future life that is conventionally held and believed by the churches. You will allow those of us who are here to speak, as to what we know, and see, and feel. And it is not what you have been conventionally taught to expect. Now I do not think that you will find that what we have to tell you differs from what the more intelligent and spiritual believers have arrived at or have received by inspiration. The fundamental principles are the same. We have nothing to tell you that was not declared by Jesus. But we have to tell you that the ideas which have been received, and are still taught by many churches as to the future state of man, are simply not correct. They make you believe what is not true. And there is no doubt at all that if you succeed in opening the Bureau that is to bridge the abyss, you will render these ideas quite unbelievable by anyone.

A Serious Danger

When you do that you run a great risk; and for this reason, these ideas, crude, raw, and false as they are, nevertheless, are probably the nearest approximation to the truth that many men can assimilate. That is what makes every transition from lower to higher truth so dangerous. Some cannot follow to the clearer statement of the same truth. And so they are lost. And when you once establish the truths of the continuity of existence, and the possibility of communication between the worlds, there will be a great gap – no, not gap – a great void left in the faith of many. This is the reason why these things are not revealed too suddenly. If you could do all that is in your mind to do at once, you would do more harm than good. It is only by slow degrees that the new truth must make its way. But that is no reason for refusing to recognize it. There must some one – be the first, and there is never any good in flinching from what is your plain duty.

No. You must go ahead, but the consolation that will sustain you when you meet with disappointments, is that if you had made more haste you would have made less speed.

The Plea for Ruts

What I want you to realize is that the great established ruts in which the truth has embedded itself cannot be destroyed without injuring for the time the truth itself. This is what I feel I must say to you. For there is too much danger that if you expect too much and forget the shadow, if you are impatient and forget the slow processes of nature, you may give it all up. And that would be a crime. I will tell you at once what the result will be. When once your Bureau is established, and when any one can get into communication with the disembodied spirits of their relatives or friends, there will be an immediate –

(Question – Disbelief in hell?)

No! You are wrong. No, the chief result will not be the abolition of the old belief in hell, for that is already abolished. People don't believe in the hell of fire of any more, and they have by their recoil forgotten that there is a real hell, which will be revealed very clearly by your Bureau. No! Please let me say what I have to say without thrusting your questions in upon my message.

The Chief Result of the Bureau

The chief change that will be made by the Bridge Bureau that you are desirous of making, will be to increase, to a quite inconceivable extent, the consciousness of the responsibility of life. You may think it strange that the verification of another life should increase the importance of this. But such is the fact, and you can never understand the importance of your life until you see it from this side. You are never, for one moment, idle from influencing eternity. You may think this a figure of speech. But it is not. You are, far more really than you imagine, making this world of ours in that world of yours.

You Make Your Own Next Life

Yes, this is a manufactured article, so to speak. You are, in the loom of time, weaving the fabric of this world. You make your next life. Yes, and you make your life here. You make your next life. You do it day by day; you do it hour by hour. You make your next life.

I wish I could express myself more clearly. You will say that this is the truth of all religions. Yes, and what all religions teach is truth; but you do not realize it, and you often deny it. If we could communicate with you, you would deny it no longer, for here, there is no sudden transformation. You are as you were. There is no break of continuity. You start where you left off. What you are you remain.

Yes, you must lot me write you what I have to say without interrupting me, as you do.

The Reign of Law Eternal

What I see will be the result of the Bureau is to immensely

deepen and strengthen the sense of the responsibility of life. This will be good, no doubt; it is what needs
strengthening. But it will not be all good. There is a danger that you wilt make the reign of law seem as inexo-
rable on this side as it is on yours, and the Fatalist will
then have Eternity as well as Time. You will see that the
will of God, which you decipher here and there as law,
stretches unbroken from your side to ours. You will find
that we, on this side, who have been able to see and feel
and know that God is Love, will also tell you that love,
no more on this side than on yours, precludes pain and
sorrow and the phenomena of imperfection. We have
not attained. We press forward to the mark of our high
calling here as there. Think you that we are transfigured
into the fullness of His glory because the earthly house
of our tabernacle is dissolved? Nay, verily. We are as we
are. When our earthly garment decays we remain. The
increase of this sense of continuity of existence of the
reign of law and of flue, responsibility of time for eternity and all that that implies, will be the greatest chancre
that your Bureau can make.

The Increase of Seriousness
There will be great and a determined seriousness of life.
There will be much more seriousness in life. There will
be no more consolation that many have taken to themselves that death ends all. Death does not end all. But it
begins much, much. But do not let me dishearten you.
There is much more good than evil. And if the Bureau
should add to the sadness of those who know not God –
for there is no escape from Him, not even in the grave –
it will make the whole universe His temple, wherein the

air, the, light, the whole, is Love.

December 12, 1896

My Dearest Friend: – When you get the Bureau of communication established you will be overwhelmed with applications from both sides.

Death as the Servant of Man

And you will find that there are multitudes who will ask for messages, but will receive none. You remember I said that I told you at the very beginning that I could either get you an answer or tell you why no communication could be established. Now there are many on this side who have been trying to get into touch with those on your side, and they have failed. You have many on your side who will make the same attempt, and who fail also. And so it will be. And so it ought to be. For there are many times when Death the Divider is the most necessary and the most useful agency that can be provided for the service of man. Nothing but evil would result if all the dead, as you call them, could haunt the living. The other world, as you call it, would be too much for you.

(Question – Then had we better not let it alone?)

No, I am quite sure that the Bureau could be a very great blessing. But it could also be a very great curse. When you have the dead hand – no, the phrase "dead hand" is not right. But it would be wiser to say that there multitudes of spirits whose removal from direct action upon the embodied living is much to be desired.

Death the Deliverer

There are multitudes of souls to whom Death has been

a great deliverance. I mean that it has taken away persons who have been harsh, cruel, and despotic. Nay, it has sometimes been kinder in removing those who have been too kind, and whose care has dwarfed, whose love and tenderness have weakened, the growing life. These influences are to be deplored which prevent the full development of the soul. But while there is little danger that the victims of tyranny and oppression will seek to reestablish relations with their oppressors who have come over to this side, there is great danger the weaklings whose staff and whose stay has gone will seek to lean again upon the support which enervated them if they can reach it through the Bureau. But there is not too much danger on that score to deter you from doing this good work. For the influence of those who live with us here in the light of the Love of the Father can only be for good.

Possible Evil of Spirit Guidance
But there are many spirits but lately disembodied whose communications, even though framed with care and inspired by love, would be mischievous and not helpful. Why, my dear friend, when you ask me for guidance, I often feel that I might be a great curse to you if I gave it you as you wish to have it. What I can do – all that I can do is to tell you how things seem to me, to remind you that while I often see more than you, you, who are living in conditions that do not prevail here, are in a better position to judge as to many things than I can be. Occasionally I am permitted to tell you things in advance for purposes of test and to give you assurance. But I should be nothing but a curse to you if I were to attempt to tell what to do. It would be like a mother always carrying a

child. It would never walk. Besides, I do not know. You must not think me omniscient because I have not got my body – my old body.

The Lesson of Self-Reliance

Oh, my friend, if you would but see and understand what is the purpose of life, you would understand how fatal it would be to allow any and every cry for direction and guidance and help to be answered. And there are many who will, if the communication be opened, forget this and give advice and will attempt to direct those who consult them, and who will make sad trouble. For it is not for us to steer you. This object of life is to evoke, to develop the God within. And that is not to be evoked by allowing others to direct you. But you will find the purpose of the Father will not be allowed to be spoiled by the folly of His children, whether on this side or on that. Those spirits that attempt to interfere too much will be confounded. They will err, and be found out. Their authority will be destroyed. And so in the end things, will come right again.

But unless you are on the look out you will find much harm will be done by the attempt of those on your side to get their thinking done for them by us. And there are many fond parents and others on this side who are only too eager to continue to exercise the authority by which they overshadowed the souls of their children on earth.

The Balance in Favor of the Bureau

Why, then, you say, should I be so anxious to get the Bureau established? Because the use of it would be so much greater than the abuse. Because you wish to have a telephone you do not want to be always rung up, or to be always told what to do. Telephones, no doubt, may easily become a nuisance. And this Bureau of mine might be a nuisance. But just think what it implies. If you could secure the communication so as to prove that life continues, that love lasts, that the other world is in contact with this – is that not enough? If it were only that, and nothing more, it would be worthwhile. Only to restore the consciousness of the invisible world and the reality of Eternal love. Only!

To Make the Unknown Known

December 31, 1896

When you are ready I will tell you more about what happens when you pass over to this side. Oh, no, I don't want to write that for this number. I was only thinking about E. (a friend, who lay dying), about her and the Unknown land. Why we want this Bureau so much is to make it a Known land. That is what you will do more and more the more you make possible the communication with this side. "The Unknown known or the truth about the Beyond. What we have to expect." That surely is what you ought to feel is worthwhile getting to know about at first hand. You will find that the spirits who will communicate to their friends through the Bureau will make very different statements. They will differ indefinitely according to their different temperaments and the manner of soul they are.

Conflicting Authorities

They will make statements which will differ so much as

to confuse those who think that the infinite multitude of individual experiences can all find a single expression. There will be any number of creeds based upon after-death experiences, which vary according to the character of the individual. The man finds this world very much what he has made it. We all make what we live in. And as everyone,

We ask for proof, and not for poet's fancies;
We hope, but with dim and starless hope,
Clouded with doubt, that evermore enhances
The dark uncertainty in which we grope.
Oh! Give us back our early faith unshaken,
That our dear dead are watching us for aye,
And know and love us, though on earth forsaken,
Soon reunited for eternal day.
No answer comes to that vain supplication,
And none will come – or ever came before,
For widow's hope or mother's consolation,
Our dead, alas! Are gone, and gone forever more.

Makes a different future life for himself they will all give you different versions of the life they lead. You will find as little uniformity here as on your side. But, nevertheless, you will find that the Bureau, and all who would use it, will agree upon certain things. They would differ endlessly about the laws, the theories, and the possibilities, but they would agree about the Facts of Being. For instance, you will not find from us on this side any authoritative declaration as to any religion that will be recognized as true by all spirits communicating. They are of all stages and phases, and the religion of some will be absolutely unthinkable by others.

The Continuity of Existence

But this you will find. There will be no spirit of any stage of development who returns to communicate through your Bureau, but will affirm that there is no breach or break in the continuity of individual existence. They will all tell you that death is a transition rather than a trans-formation, and that, although the transition is very im-portant, it in no way destroys the life of the soul. All will tell you that. All will testify to the fact that they went on living a conscious existence, that was marked off by no gulf from the life they led here. There is, no doubt, a change. But it is of circumstance rather than of charac-ter. The memory appears to be quickened rather than dulled. The mind sees more clearly.

The Unreality of Matter

The phantasmagoria of matter disappears, and the masks and masquerading that conceal the truth dissolve away – that is important and that is universal. There is not one spirit who returns, who will not assert that the mat-ter in which you are immersed is a vapor, a mere phan-tasm of the mind, which vanishes away and is not. Spirit alone is whether in the body or out of the body. And the soul lives, lives on. These two things: continuity of con-scious identity and the hollowness of matter they will all tell you are known to them, are universal facts which they will attest one and all. Where we are there can be no mistake on these points.

What you are asking I understand. Yes, I understand. What you say is true. But all spirits do not realize its truth, what I said about Love being the breath of our life is true. But what is sad is that there are multitudes here to whom it is as much an unknown thing as it is with you.

How the Bureau Might Do Harm

December 20, 1896

When you have established the Bureau, of which I have written to you so often, you will be pestered with many who will want to get into communication with those on the other side, for no good purpose. The two worlds will help each other much. But they can also hinder. And when the hindering exceeds the help, then the open door is closed. Now, I will give you instances; but please note that it will be quite as often people on our side who want to enter into communication with people on your side, for evil and not for good.

Now, there are three classes of persons who are certain to seek to communicate for their own hurt:

1 **To Those Who Have No Self-Reliance** – First, there are those whose independence of character and self-reliance has been sapped by the extent to which those who have gone overshadowed them. They will seek to be guided still, and if they succeed it will do them harm. For the benefit of what you call death is that it leaves room for the remaining ones to develop. When you get those who have been spoiled by the care and authority of parents, or guardians seeking to be guided still from beyond the Border, they will only harm themselves if they succeed. What you have to do is to grow strong and independent. What you have to avoid is to be mere shadows or echoes, or worse still, mere puppets of another will. Death has

rescued many of the living from what would have ru-
ined them. And if you open your Bureau they will try
to avoid being saved. Those who have learned to lean
will lean on the disembodied spirit, whereas they
ought to lean on themselves. Who will not trust his
own soul has lost it. And who will not rely upon the
voice of God in his own soul, will seek for it in vain in
the voices from beyond the Border.

2 **To the Idly Curious** – Secondly, the second class of
persons to whom your Bureau will be mischievous
is composed of those who are merely curious. Mere
busybodies, with an inquisitive itch, will come to ask
from no deep longing for knowledge of the other side,
from no real desire to communicate with the departed. They will throng your Bureau as they would go
to a dime museum and put a penny in the Slot to get
some novelty. They will get no good. They are not serious. They merely come from motives of curiosity
and a love of sensation. They will get no good. They
may get harm.

3 **To Partners in Sin** – Thirdly, there are those who
are by no means so few in number, who will wish to
perpetuate a sinful relationship. They will not admit
this. Put they will seek it earnestly, desperately more
often than you imagine. And it may be granted them.
The alliance that had been severed by the grave may
be resumed. Yes, this is possible and is done. There
is a possibility of the resumption of relations, which
you believed had been severed forever by death. There
is danger here, and it is a danger against which you
must be on your guard. Therefore, I say, do not think
that the Bureau will be an unmixed good! Much as

I desire its establishment, I see that for many it will work almost unmixed evil.

Men will find what they bring. And the majority of men will seek not good, but what they desire.

Now, the desire of men is by no means always for that which is highest and best.

(Question – Then, do you think we had better drop the idea?)

But Still Establish the Bureau

My dear friend, what nonsense you talk! Do you propose to drop navigation because you hear of storms and rocks and quicksand? No! No! No. What is necessary is to recognize that the Borderland is as important (at least) as crossing as the Atlantic, but that it is not any safer. What you seem to forget is that the Bureau, with all its risks, will do what is the most important thing of all. It will practically abolish the conception of death, which now prevails in the world. You have become mere materialists. We must break through the wall of matter, which is stifling your souls. And the Bureau will make a way for the light from beyond to shine through. That is enough to justify the facing of any risks, such as I have described.

Yes, the New Year will be with you soon, and I hope that it will not close without some serious effort being made to establish that Bureau, of which I have written so much. Avoid as much as possible the these classes of whom I have written, and confine your attention and concentrate your efforts upon the verification of the continuity of existence, and the possibility of securing unmistakable communications from those who have passed the Borderland.

Now, goodbye. Julia.

5

The Open Door to the Open Secret

The following message is printed as received, with interlocutory observations by the transmitter in parenthesis. The statements which are made are capable of verification, but the assertions contained in this message are certainly not such as I should have dreamed of making on my own authority; and even on Julia's as will be seen, I hesitated about publishing them, and only did so on the assurances of two independent investigators that, much to my surprise, Julia's message embodied what they regard as indubitable truth. W. T. S.

March 14, 1897

My Dearest Friend: – I am very anxious to give you the message that I spoke of when I last wrote. We have been very interested in the recent manifestations of the apparitions of which you have so much to tell and to hear. But we are not satisfied with any of them. Where they occur they are so fitful and uncertain, they are practically worthless.

What is Wanted?
Now what we want to prove is, that when you conform to the laws governing Borderland, there is no more reason why you should not have apparitions as regularly and as certainly as you have light when you strike a match. Because, as you know, the apparitions are there all the time, only they do not appear. That is nothing

but a difference of the focus of the eye. When you have a focus adjusted only to see material things, you can only see material things. But when you are able to adjust your focus at will, you will be able to see what there is to be seen; and that with as much certainty as the astronomer sees through his telescope stars invisible to the naked eye. As the heavens are strewn thick with unsuspected worlds, so all around is full of beings which are as real as the smaller or more distant stars. When you look for the stars in the glare of noonday they are not to be seen; but they are there all the time. And so it is with the masses of mankind. We are all around you, without you seeing or feeling our presence. And I am not sure that, as a rule, for the mass of human beings, it is not better that they do not see. The mariner who steers by the familiar constellations might lose his way if the dim invisible stars revealed by the telescope were suddenly to become equally visible to him as the others.

To See the Invisible at Will
But all that we want is that those of you who can, should be able to see at will those beings which are normally invisible to the naked eye. I do not know whether you will always relish this consciousness of your existing, as it were, under perpetual supervision. And then the Beings, which you will see when your eyes are adjusted to the Borderland, are by no means always agreeable, nor are they always calculated to help you to live the life that is highest. These things exist on both sides. And you may say, "Where ignorance is bliss, 'tis folly to be wise." But more are they that are for you than all those that can be against you; and the opening up of the new vista will

not weaken but strengthen, if you are strong and do not fear. Waves, which drown the timorous, are helpers of the brave. And in Borderland there are many waves.

(Question – But what is the message?)

The Sixth Sense

Well, do not be impatient. What I have to tell you is, that all those who really wish to have the sixth sense, or whatever you term it, so developed that they can, at will, become sensibly, or through their senses, cognizant of the reality of the existence of the beings who encompass them about, can acquire the gift or faculty if they will but adapt themselves to the laws of the region into which they wish to penetrate.

(Question – Everybody?)

Yes, it is a potentiality of the universal human race. Nor is it only human. Many animals have the open eye. They see, when their owners are blind. But you can see if you choose. It all rests with yourselves.

(Question – Well, tell me how?)

Yes, that is what I am coming to. What you want is a prescription, a kind of apothecary's pill, to purge away the dullness that darkens your eye. My friend, that is impossible. I have no such pill. The road is one that must be traversed. The lessons must be learned. The laws must be obeyed. And that is not a matter of prescription, or potion, or charm.

No, there is no short cut to the sixth sense. There may be something like it in mesmerism and hypnotism; but that is not all that I mean. What is possible is for every child of man to become what you call normally clairvoyant. That is, for any one to possess himself of the power of seeing and hearing, as plainly as he sees and hears material things, the invisible forms and voices that surround you.

Must be Under Control

The power is one that ought to be under control. There would be only harm done if you could not shut at will the clairvoyant eye. Imagine the mischief that would happen if, when life and death hung on the absolute concentration of all faculties on the subject immediately before you, if at the supreme moment you were to see the whole phantasmagoria of Borderland pass between you and the point of exclusive attention. If you cannot control your sixth sense you had better not acquire it; better be without it than be controlled by it. You should have it at command when you need it, as you have your microscope or your telescope. But better have neither if you were to be compulsorily doomed at other will than yours, to interrupt the work of life by the spectacle of the infinitely little or the infinitely remote. Man should always be master or his senses, especially of the sixth (so-called).

The Unseen

March 15, 1897

Now let me begin by stating, once for all, that the secret things of the world are those which are the most common, the most universal, the most important. It is not things seen which are eternal. The secret forces of what you call material nature, gravitation, heat, electricity, ether, everything, in short, which is anything, is the unseen and yet universal. So it is with the spiritual entities which are all around, and which you can demonstrate the existence of as unfailingly as the existence of these other invisible things I have just spoken of.

The Three Requisites

But as in any research you must equip yourself with tools and instruments; so in this it is necessary for you to be provided with such things as are necessary. And the first indispensable is that you should have the heart of a little child. There is no one who will enter into the kingdom who has not got the heart of a little child. That does not mean that it must be ignorant, but that it must always be simple, and must always think first of what it perceives and not always of itself. The intense self-consciousness of age, the constant questioning as to how this or that will affect yourself, and not simply what it is, will play havoc with the chances of your success. When you have determined to approach the phenomena, or whatever you call it, in a spirit of a child, you have the first desideratum. The second is not unlike. You must not only have the heart of a child, but you must have the keen reason and common sense of a man. There are plenty of illusions, and there are many pitfalls. You need all your mental faculties. Be vigilant, accept everything as a child does; but examine and test everything as a man does, without prejudice and without partiality. And the third requirement is patience. Nothing can be achieved without time and patience. But if you have the heart of a little child, the mind of man, and the patience that, being fed by hope, never wearies, you will have the three essentials.

The Love Motive

There is another thing that I might have mentioned. And that is what lies under and over and around you. It is Love. If you do not enter upon this quest, prompted by love, I do not say that you will not succeed – if the laws are followed you will – but it will make all the difference to your results and to the comfort and peace you will have in attaining them, if you pursue the investigation from a love motive and not from mere cold curiosity. Love of truth is good. But you will find that when to love of abstract truth there is added a spirit longing for communion with other spirits who are on this side, the double current is more potent. And your results will be better. You can grow flowers in the tropics or in the arctic regions; but the flowers are brighter and more easily cultivated in the tropics than amid the snow. And in all spiritual things the temperature depends upon Love.

Physical Conditions

And now, having spoken of the mental qualifications, let me speak next of the physical. When you are setting about the investigation, you may not be in good health, and you may succeed notwithstanding. But the odds are heavily against the diseased or the infirm, in this as in all pursuits requiring attention, energy of mind and courage. The best-equipped investigator may be paralyzed by a physical ailment. What I have to say on this subject is nothing new. Practise the laws of health. Wash yourself, and keep yourself clean! While many dirty saints have seen visions, they would have had clearer vision had they had cleaner skins. Take exercise; live not to eat, but eat to live. No, I make no restrictions upon diet. Bat what makes you most efficient. There is only one rule about food and drink. Use it.

(Question – Then you don't insist on vegetables?)

No, I do not think for the purpose that I have in view, it is well to insist upon vegetarian diet. If you had been always a vegetarian, that would be different. It might, and possibly would, be better for you. But for you, and all those who are accustomed to a mixed diet, to become vegetarians in order to be better clairvoyants would not be wise. For your health would suffer so much in the period when you were being accustomed to the new diet, the loss would be greater than the gain. And, on the same principle, I do not think that for married people there is any duty of abstinence from conjugal union as a condition of success. There must never be union without love. But when there is perfect love and perfect union there is a nearer approach to the perfect existence, which, as one of its elements, has the clairvoyant gift.

March 17, 1897

We will now begin the more special part of what I have to say to you. What I have said is only the general rule of life, and it is as useful for any one as for the psychic student. All may be summed up in one word, viz., Live and Love. Now for the particular message that I have to give you, and, through you, to the readers of *Borderland.*

Observation by Recipient

(Now here I may as well interrupt my contributor by saying that I have not any glimmering of an idea as to what she is going to say. I fear that I am very skeptical about it. I distinctly do not believe that it will be so easy or certain

113

as she says to reveal the Invisible. I may, of course, be wrong. I can never forget that when Julia told me about automatic writing with living people I was almost as skeptical, but she was right then, and she may be right now. But the odds seem to be very heavy against it. I hope that I may be wrong. But if anything is given to me that at all corresponds to the sweeping announcement with which this message was begun, I think it only right to put on record the fact that my physically conscious mind is absolutely a blank on the subject. I cannot even form any kind of imagination what she is going to say.)

No, I know that is so. Sometimes I am able to impress your physically conscious mind, and I do so. Sometimes I cannot. Sometimes I might, but I prefer not to. This is one of the last cases.

Be Alone

Now the first thing to be got is a place where you can be alone. Enter into thy closet! Solitude, exclusion from the world of sense, that is the first thing. When thou hast shut the door, remain alone for a time, long enough to allow the waves of the world's thoughts and cares to subside. Sometimes you could be quiescent and passive in a very few minutes. But at other times you could not regain the tranquil mood in any number of minutes. When you are about to verify this message you must be at peace. When you are in a whirl, or are in a bitter mood, or when the mind goes on and on creaking round and round like a wheel that is not greased, don't try. But when your health is good, when your mind is calm, and your mood is quite serene and happy, then go into your closet and shut the door.

(Question – And close the window-shutters?)

You need not darken the room, unless the sight of the contents or the view from the windows distracts mind and prevents the concentration of the attention. But it is probable that at first, if you are not very restful, a shaded room would be better.

And Be Still

When you are alone and still, and the door is locked, so that no one can disturb you, sit as easily as you can so as to be as far as possible unconscious of any physical discomfort or anything that reminds you of your body.

(Question – Sit and not kneel?)

I do not recommend you to kneel. The posture is not convenient for long, and any posture that reminds you that it is a posture is wrong. What you have to do is to avoid reminders from the other senses of their existence.

(Question – Why not lie down?)

I do not advise you to lie down because it suggests sleep, and I do not wish to confuse the revealing of the Invisible with the visions of the dreamer. Sit, therefore, as easily as possible, and as far as possible also avoid everything that will remind you of your body.

Objection by the Recipient

(Now here I interrupt again, to say that it seems as if she were about to recommend some kind of self-hypnotization. Some fakir-like gazing at the tip of your nose, or something or other like that, which I don't like – and as far as I have formed an opinion or a prejudice I don't believe in. So far all that she has said seems practical, simple

enough, but – but – . Well, now I will let her proceed.)

A Well-Deserved Rebuke

What an impatient unbeliever you are! What you like or don't like does not matter much, does it? What you want to know are the laws by which you must abide if you wish to avoid failure. Tides are inconvenient very often, but the wise mariner does not indulge in prejudice against tides. Listen, I am not wasting your time. I have this to tell you, and if you will do as I direct you will have the results. If not, there is no compulsion. You wish to see me, for instance, and to hear me, instead of merely reading what I write. You will both see and hear and touch me if you will obey my instructions, and not interrupt with your likings and dislikings, which, after all, are not important.

An Interruption

When you are alone in the darkened room – for you better try it with shade at first – then you must do this.

(Here the writing broke off. Then in another handwriting came:)

The good angel of guidance will come again, and you will be told all. At present you must stop. No more now. Never mind.

March 18, 1897

I am so sorry that I had to leave you yesterday. But there was an urgent call for me elsewhere. So I had to go. But now I am with you again, I will resume where I left off.

The first thing to be done, if you would have your eyes opened to see the invisible ones who surround you, is to be very still. As I said, make no effort. Be still and wait. You need to be quite passive, so as to let the other world outside slacken its hold on you, and the real world within and around you make itself felt.

How to Proceed

Then, when you are quite still and passive, close your eyes and think of the one whom you wish to see. If it is a friend still alive, in the body, it will help you if at the same time, although that is not essential, he or she were also to be passive and alone. When you have two spirits in accord, both seeking the same thing, the difficulties are less. But you must be agreed. One must wish to manifest, the other to be manifested to. And during the seclusion do not change the parts. Close your eyes, and, in the absence of the outside, imagine as quietly and distinctly as possible your friend. If he is to come to you, think of him steadily, concentrating your thought on him and him alone. Think of him in detail. Make a thought-image of him, as if you were actually creating him. And all the while let your heart and soul go out in a steady longing for him to come. At the same time let him, wherever he may be, be also alone sitting with closed eyes, willing steadily to come to you wherever you may be. Let him, on his part, think of some simple heartfelt message to you. Let it be on his tongue to say it; not loudly, but with quiet, earnest confidence that you will hear. Let him repeat it quietly with the wish that you should hear it. That is all.

A Promise

If you, or any two who are in accord, will do that, do it

steadily in the right spirit, you will be able to see each other and to hear each other speak. It is not to be done in a day, except in rare psychics, who are in absolute accord. But if you try it for yourselves, you will see that I have spoken the truth, just as you did about the automatic handwriting from living persons. This requires more effort than the other. There are no difficulties but those of excluding the rushing, distracting flood of cares and worries. Be alone; be silent; be in a mood to receive, and you will be able to verify what I say.

(Question – How long must this abstraction continue? And how often must it be tried before there is any reasonable hope of success?)

Everything depends upon the nature of the person and the extent to which he can distract his attention from the things of this world. As you know, there have been within your knowledge cases where the Double of a living person has come in response to appeals both from the sleeping and from those who are awake, without any Ion abstraction. But at first there is a possibility that the unusual effort may in itself distract. You will think so much of the effort as to be unable to think of the friend.

Never Force Things

There is no hard-and-fast rule. I should say that the best general rule is never to force things. If you are tired in five minutes, stop then. If you can keep up the concentrated, quiet attention for a longer period, do so. But remember, the sense of strain is bad. There must be no strain; there must be no effort. Only passive readiness to see. Do not make the mistake of imagining that intensity of muscular or mental will tension is what is wanted. It is the reverse of that. Be still, and listen and watch. You must be guided by your own experiences. If you suffer in any way, drop it. If it distracts your thoughts from your daily work, do not touch it. But if you acquire this power, and have it under control as a constant possession, for you parting will be no more; unless, of course, there is a mental breach. But that is not what people mean by parting.

(Question – But is this not only a sustained effort of the imagination? Is there objectivity in the image thus created in the dark?)

The Form Not Subjective

What is imagination? If you see only what you willed to see, your objection would bold. But, if having imagined your friend in a grey suit he should appear to you in a brown, or if the image which you have imagined should speak, telling you what you did not know, but what your friend was at that moment saying to you, would that be imagination only? No, what I have said is true. You can secure the living presence of the friend with whom you are in close accord if you will but adopt these simple rules.

(Question – Humph; I wonder – ?)

They are so simple you do not like them, I see. You would have preferred something more magical – more out of the way. But there is no need for these wrappings. The simple truth is that you all have the capacity to do this if only you would use your souls instead of being immersed in your material bodies.

(Question – But will the image not be a mere clairvoyant vision, seen with closed eyes?)

But a Tangible Reality

At first, as a rule, it will be so. But after a time you, or at least some of you, will be able to materialize it sufficiently for it to be visible to the physical eye in broad day. Others may not see the person who is to you visible, audible, and touchable. But you will be conscious of his presence.

(Question – Then does the same rule hold good as to the spirits of the disembodied?)

Yes; only there are differences. With the disembodied, for instance, you cannot, as it were, check the accuracy of the psychic sense by the impressions of material things and the physical consciousness. That is why it is better to begin with the spirit of the embodied. But spirit is spirit everywhere, and the accident of its embodiment does not render it easier or more difficult to communicate.

A Neglected Heritage

Oh, my friend, how I do wish you would but open your eyes and see. You are living in a cell whereas you might go out and occupy and possess the whole, world. Why should you, with a heritage which I have faintly endeavored to describe, live only in the material senses? Why, when you can defy time and space, and live with any of your friends, no matter how far you may be severed, should you live and think and act as if you were confined to the narrow cell bounded by your physical consciousness? Ali that it needs is to be alone, to be silent, to be passive. But, of course, you must not imagine that all this unseen world of spirit, which is now opening before you, can be taken possession of in a moment. There are many things to be learned, many stages to be passed through. But make a beginning; and know that what you know of the reality of the Double, which at present goes like the wind where it listeth, is for you a sign and a pledge of the possibility of making the sense- world appear but as a dungeon compared with the immense possibilities of the Spirit.

6

On the Losing and the
Finding of the Soul

July 11, 1897

My Dearest Friend: – What I am now going to write is for *Borderland.*

(I have not a ghost of an idea what it is to be about.)

Oh, what an opportunity you have this year of making a memorable and permanent memento of the Queen's Jubilee.

(Question – Humph! Does the Jubilee interest you?)

Yes, we are interested in this as in all that stirs the heart and moves the soul of man. We see what you are thinking, and we see what you are doing. And we see also what you ought to do if you would but use the opportunity aright. And that is what I want to write with your hand today.

(Personally, I rather resent Julia's intervention with Jubilee affairs. The feeling may be absurd, but I wish she would riot mix herself up in this business.)

Yes, I know, but when I have to say things, what you like or dislike does not matter. What I have to tell you is that the Jubilee gives you a great chance of effecting permanent good. All that you have done has been well done and useful. But you have now to begin the real Jubilee.

My Message or Julia's?

You have to make up for the self-jubilation and vainglory of pride and power by humbling yourselves before the Giver of all these gifts. Otherwise you will not have long to wait for the humiliation to come.

(This is what I have said already myself.)

Oh, why will you not let me write quietly and leave your objections? I will say what I have to say, and you can object afterwards. But let me say at once that you will find it very difficult to distinguish between what you say yourself and what we impress upon your mind. But now that I am writing, please let me write without interruption.

What I want to say is that the people at large will be more receptive to the truth now than they were before. The Jubilee was a great mind-waker. And when the mind is wakened up your work is half done. What you have to do is to go through the open door which stands wide before you; and if you will but let me have my say without these restless questionings and objections, I think you will admit I have something to say which you have not said, but which I hope you will say hereafter. What you have said about a revival is good; but I wish to point out to you how that revival can be brought about.

All that is to be told would take a long time. But there are some things which can be said quite briefly, which you will see are not at all your ideas.

The Worst Evil of the Day

First of all, what you need to think of above everything else in regard to this matter is, what you or any one of you are doing to make the Real World real to men. The worst evil of the present day is not its love of money, nor its selfishness. No, but its Loss of the Soul. You forget that the soul is the thing. And that all that concerns the body, except so far as it affects the Soul, is of no importance. But what you have to realize is that men and women in this generation have lost their souls. And this is a terrible truth. It is not what we used to think of losing the Soul in hell, after laying aside the body. It is a thing not of the future only, but of the present. Your Soul is lost now. And you have to find it.

What Lost Soul Means
When I say lost, I mean it. You have lost it as you might lose a person in a crowd. It is severed from you. You are immersed in matter and you have lost your Soul. And the first, the most pressing of all things, is to find your Soul. For until you find it you are little better than an active automaton, whose feverish movements have no real significance, no lasting value. The Loss of the Soul, that is the Malady of the Day; and to find the Soul is the Way to Salvation.

How the Soul Has Been Lost
The finding of the Soul is the first thing and the most important thing. You will never find it unless you give yourself time to think, time to pray, time to realize that you have a soul. At present, then, do you remember that? You remember when you must catch trains. But when do you remember that you must catch your Soul? No, no! All is rush, and jump, and whirl, and your Soul gets lost, crowded out of your life. You have so many engagements that you have no time to live the Soul-life. That is what

124

you have to learn. No doubt your work is important, and duty must be done. But what shall it profit a man if he gain the whole world and lose his own Soul?

The Soul of the Nation and of the Individual

The way the Jubilee helps is that that the ordinary man has discovered that there is something he seldom thought of which he now sees is most important. He has at least got a glimpse of the Soul of the Nation, and sees the greatness of the sight. Now teach him that it is even more important to find his own soul – the lost Soul which he has crowded out of his life.

You understand that? You grasp that?

How to Find the Soul

Now I will go to speak as to, how to find the Soul.

There is only one way. There is no chance of salvation if you never give yourself time to think on things that are timeless, that transcend time, that will be when time shall be no more.

You have no time but for the things of time which perish with the using. And if you would find your Soul you must give time to the search.

You say you have no time. But you have time to make money, to amuse yourself, to make love, to do anything that you really want to do. But your Soul, that is a thing you do not care about. And so you have no time for the Soul.

You are getting less and less spiritual. The old ordinances, the services, the prayers, the meditation, the retreat, these gave you time. But one by one they all go – these cases where you could rest and meet your Soul.

And you have materialized yourself even with the fretful struggle against materialism. For what is more important than struggling to stem evil is to save your Soul, to possess your Soul, to hold it and not let it go.

The Importance of the Soul

What seems to me quite clear is that the indifference to the Soul is caused by not understanding that the Soul is the Real Self, the only part of you which lasts, the Divine in you, which you are sacrificing to the things of the day.

What you do not understand is that it is through the Soul alone that you can commune with the Spiritual World that is all around you. And the Spiritual World includes the entire world excepting the perishing things of time. When we say Spiritual World we include what you call God and His Holy Angels and the sainted dead. All these are lost to you when you lose your Soul. For the Soul alone communicates with the Real World.

It is through the Soul you obtain inspiration. The Soul links you with the Universe of God with the Soul of the World. And when you lose touch with your Soul you become a mere prisoner in the dungeon of matter, through which you peer a little way by the windows of the senses.

(That is what all religions always say, and will the mere saying of it again do any good?)

What all religions say is true. But what I say is a little different. Not to what all religions have said, but to what materialized religions say now. And therein lies the difference.

Its Divine Powers

For what I say is that the Soul has Divine powers, but if you will but find your Soul, and develop its Divine potency, there is opened before you a new heaven and a new earth, in which Absence is not, nor Death, and, where the whole Universe of Love is yours.

(Question – Miracles, then?)

Yes, I maintain that what you call miracles are the natural capacities of the Soul. Miracles of Healing, Miracles of Movement, Miracles of Power, which you little dream of, are within the scope of the Soul. All that you have read of about the power of Spirit over Matter is nothing to the reality. You are as caterpillars to what you might be.

But the doorway into the Infinite is the Soul, and the Soul is lost. When you have no time to think, no time to pray, you have no time to live. Therefore you must before all else make time.

(Easier said than done!)

Make Time!

Oh, my dear friend, why are you so skeptical? You waste more time in brooding over the past which you cannot recall, or in anticipating the evils of the Future which you may never meet, than would help you to possess your Soul in the living Present.

What you do not seem to see is that the Soul is not a mere abstraction. It is the power which enables you to do all things.

I speak the most sober and literal truth, when I say that if you did but possess your Soul and exercise its powers, Death or separation in this world would cease to exist for you, and the miseries which haunt the human race would disappear.

The Cause of Misery

For the whole of the evils that afflict society arise from the lack of seeing things from the standpoint of the Soul. If you lived for the Soul, cared for what made the Soul a more living reality, and less for the meat and drink and paraphernalia of the body, the whole world would be transfigured; you have got a wrong standpoint and everything is out of focus.

I do not say neglect the body. But make its health and ease only the means to the end. The body is only a machine. The work that it does ought to be for the Soul. What you do now is to make the machine everything. The wheels go round, but nothing moves. And in the whirl of the wheels the Soul is lost

Losing the Soul by Seeking to Save It

No! I must repeat once more – you must find time to live. At present you have lost your Souls even partly by the strain of trying to find them. I mean that much of the so-called religious life and works, while good in their way, constitutes no small addition to the preoccupation of time which renders Soul-life impossible to lose your Soul in church as well as life impossible. It is possible to lose your Soul in church as well as on the exchange. If you have no leisure to be alone with your Soul – it does not so much matter whether the rush and whirl and preoccupation is ecclesiastical or financial – the Soul is lost, and there is nothing to do but to find it again.

Make the Soul the Center

You may sum up what I have to say in one or two words. What I wish you to do is to make the Soul the center, and make time to use the Soul, which alone can do all things. Make Time to save Eternity, nay, to possess it now and to know God.

7

Parting Words

September 19,1897

My Dearest Friend: – My heart is somewhat sad within me at the thought that this may be the last time for some months that I shall have the much-prized opportunity of communicating with my friends, whom I have so often addressed through the pages of *Borderland.* It is now nearly four years since I began to write for them, and I have had much blessed evidence as to the help which my letters have given to many who had otherwise almost despaired.

Her Parting Word

Now that for the present, and only for the present, my letters must cease, I feel more than ever impressed with the importance of insisting once more, more strongly than ever before, on the great truth that God is Love, and that all who love really and truly are in God and He in them. I have said this many times. But you do not seem to realize how literally true it is, and bow absurd it will seem to you when you come over here and see how God has been kept out of your lives because of the lack of love in your hearts. There is nothing in all the worlds so true, so vital, so universal as this. Love and God are the same, and when, from any cause, you hate or do not love, to that extent you shut God out from your life.

If I had only one message to give, this is the message – Love.

On Being as God

If you would be as God, love! Everything you love is a step toward heaven. Everything you dislike so as to make you incapable of loving any one, takes you down the steps away from Him. You think that it is righteous to be wrath, and you do, well. But although you may be righteous and wrath, you cannot be at one with God if your wrath makes you to be out of charity with the offender. You may punish the offender – but in love. If you love to punish, if the pain you inflict pleases you – beware! You are out of love, and to be out of love is to be out of the very Being of God.

(Question – But does this not result in spoiling people?)

On Punishing

No; this is not to spoil people. Be just, nay, even be sternly just. You do not neglect to punish your child because you love him. But the pain you inflict is felt first by yourself. You cannot punish another rightly but you must bear it upon your own heart first. All bitterness, all desire for vengeance, all hardening of the heart that causes you not to feel the pain you must inflict upon another; these things are contrary to love and, therefore, are enemies of God. Love is not more yielding to pleasant, easygoing complacency or indifference; that is not love, but self-love. The love that spoils a child is cruel as hate. It is selfishness. You must often smite in love. But love feels the blow before it is delivered: suffers first and feels the most. This is one of the many, the innumerable lessons of the Passion of our Lord.

On the Gain of Death

When I have written of late months I have not said so much as I did in my earliest letters about the spirit-life and the ever blessed realities of our union with Him who is Love, and with whom to be is heaven. But there is nothing that I wrote that I have to unsay. Rather, if I could, would I repeat it all over again, more earnestly, more lovingly than ever. The greatest, the most delightful, the only important thing, compared with which all other things are as nothing, is that by what you call Death we have come into a far closer, more intimate realization of His presence, of His Life in us, and our Life in Him. All that we can say, all that has been but as faint and imperfect symbols.

On the Love of God

Oh, my friend, my friend, you know not, nor can I ever pretend to begin to explain the exceeding wonder, and glory, and infinitude of the sense of the realized Love of God for us, in which we live, and move, and have our being. I wish that I could make you feel it more. I wish I could explain it better. But I cannot say more than that – it is more than I ever dreamed of, more, far more, than I tried to explain in my first letters. All that you know of earthly love – the love of mother for her child, the love of bridegroom for bride, the love of husband and wife – all earthly loves and ecstasies of affection, are but as the alphabet of the language of heaven. And the more ideally and unselfishly you love, the more you understand

God and have God in you, the hope of glory. What the glories of sunrise are to the grey twilight that precedes dawn is our life of love to the life you lead, excepting in those high moments when the heart glows with a divine exaltation which is born of the inspiration and consecration of love.

On the Vision of God

Alas, how feeble are my words! I cannot utter what I feel. I only know that when you will know you will feel as powerless as myself to explain.

Now, this is why I am always saying to you, Love, Love, Love! Because the difference between your side and this side is chiefly in this – there is more love here, as there is more sunshine in summer than in winter. If there were but more love in your world it would be even as ours; for to you also would be given the Vision of God. And that brings one to another truth, which I would fain once more insist upon before I close my letter.

On the Last Enemy

Your world is not at all so hopeless as you think. You have far more Divine attributes than you imagine. The worst of your world is the want of love. If there were love where there is hatred or indifference, earth would become heaven. Even your most skeptical people admit that. But they say that even with love there would be the anguish of parting and the misery of death, and while this is so, who increases love increases sorrow, for the closer the tendrils twine the more anguish it causes to tear them off.

And that is why I have ever been so insistent upon the

fact that if you will but cultivate your souls and cease to immerse yourselves in inert matter you will be able to triumph over the last enemy. For you who have so imperfectly, and at such irregular intervals, made proof of what I say, know that it is often possible, even to you whose life is so engrossed with worldly cares and pressing duties, to communicate or to receive communications from friends far away of so intimate and constant a nature that they throw into the shade all speech and correspondence.

Gleams of the Coming Day

You know also, from the experience of friends, that the possibilities of the multiplication of person, the creation of the apparent Double of one's body, and its transport to any place with the speed of thoughts, is no mere fantasy of the imagination. These things with you are fitful gleams of the coming day. They can be, as I have told you, developed until parting will be no more, and the greatest drawback to the increase of love will vanish away.

There is no sense that shall not be satisfied, no demonstration of the reality of this latent energy of spirit that shall be wanting. The spirit that takes no heed of the limitations and trammels, of the body when the body lives is not less free when the body is laid in the grave. The power that creates a Double can cause the living who love to receive their dead again.

(But all these years I have never seen you.)

An Objection to a Reproof

Now, my dearest friend, it is true as you object that you have never seen me since I passed over. But when the water is disturbed there is no reflection of your face. There must be a calm and placid surface even for a mirror. And how often have you been calm and placid, tranquilly waiting for the manifestation of the Invisible?

You know that, though you have not seen me with your own eye, others have, and that under circumstances which preclude deception. And if you have not seen me, have you not had constant witness of my presence in messages and communications which have never failed these five years?

(But, perhaps, after all, they may have been –)

Julia on the Evidence of Her Existence

Oh, I know well the skeptical doubt. These messages which you have received at all times and seasons; of which possibly a hundredth part have been published in *Borderland,* may, you suggest, have been due solely to your sub consciousness, your other self. Your hand which has written things unknown to you which have occurred in the past, and which has written things as yet unknown to any one which have been fulfilled in the future, is, moved not by me but by some hitherto unknown segment of your soul. Well, you can take it so if you please. But you know, best of all, whether these communications, many of which ran directly counter to your own views, and all of which form a consistent whole with a distinct character and individuality of their own, did, or did not, emanate from your own mind. They certainly did not emanate from your conscious mind; and if you know nothing of their contents, you know nothing of their origin. I, who know both, have always told you the same thing. I am your old friend on earth-life who passed away some five years ago, and who has ever since been with you to teach, to console, and to assist you in direction.

When we speak of death as separation, has it separated us? Have I not been more constantly, more faithfully, more intimately with you than ever was possible to me when on earth? Then, if that is so, and you know it is true, why should you doubt that it can be so with all mortals? For what one attains is a measure of the latent possibilities of all beings.

I have often regretted that you did not take more particular steps to establish the Bureau of which I have been too impatient. The times and the seasons are not revealed to us, even here. But it will come, and when it comes you will understand. Julia.

Fragments

(The following fragment was begun on April 12, 1897. It has not yet been finished. I include it chiefly because of its concluding passage.)

The Truth of Life: Here and Hereafter
By One Who Has Lived on Both Sides

Life at Birth

April 12, 1897

When man first finds himself conscious of life he is purely animal. There may be in him the breath of God. But his consciousness is limited to the wants of his animal nature. He has hunger and thirst. He is warm or cold, and beyond these things he has no consciousness worth speaking of. He has not even sight, as we understand it. For the art of seeing is not an innate art. We see, but we do not understand what we see until experience has taught us how to distinguish and how to connect shapes with certain sights. He hears, but all that he hears is vague noises which he cannot distinguish one from the other. But that is what life is to the newborn child. A sense of hunger and cold, of warmth, of thirst, a capacity to suffer if his skin is bruised or scratched, with a certain dull perception of light and sound. That is the beginning of life in the world for man. Wherein there lies a parable and an allegory.

A Parable and an Allegory

For what the infant with its five senses of sensation, what the infant with its purely rudimentary animal consciousness is to the full-grown man, to Plato, to Shakespeare, to Newton, that the full-grown man in the highest stage of his development on earth is to the man as he is capable of becoming when he leaves his body and becomes a denizen of the other world. All that you know and feel and understand is but as the beginning of things. It corresponds strictly to the simple consciousness in the newly born. It is a beginning, a germ, a prophecy of things to be, the basis and foundation for that which is to come.

Difficulty of Explanation

Now as the full grown finds it impossible to explain the conceptions of philosophy or of science to the child in the cradle, so it is impossible for those of us who have attained to the life beyond to explain so that you can understand the fuller life which lies before the human race. Hence, when I have undertaken to tell you the Truth about Life here and hereafter, I do not mean that I shall tell you all the truth even as I perceive it, much less all the truth that is to be perceived hereafter. For we never fully attain to the knowledge of all truth. All that I can tell you is conditioned in two ways; first, by the limits of my own knowledge; and, secondly, by the possibilities of your own capacity to receive and understand. But, subject to these limitations, I will explain all things that it is useful and needful for you to know.

The Advantage of the Standpoint

I have not got any startling revelations to make. But I

think that it may be helpful to you to know how life appears to us, for as it appears to us now, so it will appear to you hereafter. There is always an advantage in looking at your life work from a point a little removed or outside yourself. You make fewer deviations from the true line when you glance along the way you have traveled from a fixed point behind to the goal towards which you are aiming. You are always in danger of missing your way. You are liable to mistake the main road, or passage, and to stray into byways which lead nowhither. The problem of life is surely to avoid the waste of straying into *culs-de-sacs* or being led into devious ways which do not help you forward. In other words, what you have to do is to see the point towards which you are tending and to persistently press towards it.

Prepare for That Which is to Come

You need to accumulate strength for faculties that will be used. It is no use spending life in developing a sense that will not be needed hereafter. If you were to spend your life on the sea, the obvious duty of those who educated you would be to prepare you for the seafaring life. And so, when you come to this side, your first thought will be of the waste of life that has gone on in the past. Waste of opportunities, waste of strength, waste of growth, for the conditions of life, the object of existence, here are so different that to many the first impression is that of bankruptcy. They have spent their life in accumulating treasure, and so the deposits in the bank on the other side cannot be drawn here, and they are undone.

(I objected that this was but the old text about laying

up treasures where moth and rust do not corrupt or thieves break through and steal.)

The Old, Old Story

Yes, I know, and if you think that I am going to tell you anything that has not been told many times already by those who have gone out from this side to teach you on that, you are very much mistaken. "Lay not up for yourselves treasures where moth and rust doth corrupt and where thieves do break through and steal," is a maxim which you have heard often enough; but do you attend to it? I have only to repeat it with new accents and to tell you that the testimony of all of us is the same. It is the things unseen which are eternal and the things invisible which are alone of value. And my object is to urge you to concentrate life in the body on objects that will last after you reach this side, and not on those which cease to profit after death.

April 13

What I wrote yesterday was a kind of preface. Now I am going to write straight on, just what my message is.

On Life Here

Life here is sensation and consciousness of Being. And the more you analyze it the more you will come back to this. Sensation and consciousness of Being are the two signs of life. And they continue as long as man lives.

Now sensation is a thing of the outward mechanism in which the spirit lives.

Pre-Existence of Soul

What you have to realize is that the Soul was before the birth of the body and continues after the body is dissolved. All that is needed in that body is a mechanism whereby under the physical conditions the incarnate soul may acquire the experience necessary to its evolution. The conditions of that mechanism are sensation and consciousness. The consciousness is needed in some cases not continuous with life. The mechanism sometimes lives on where consciousness manifesting through the body appears to be extinct. There is, for instance, no consciousness of existence during sound sleep. But life continues. And the senses feel even in sleep. What I am trying to do is to explain life.

And I say as I began, Life is sensation and consciousness of Being.

The Two Signs of Life

When sensation ends, death of the body begins. There is no such thing as death of the soul, at any rate at the physical stage of its development. What there may be hereafter I may speak of hereafter, but not now. What you call life is sensation and a consciousness of being occasioned by the sense of sensation.

(I became somewhat impatient, not seeing what she was driving at.)

I am going on all right; only your mind is anything but passive. Wait and see what I have to write, you are so skeptical. What I have to tell you is my affair. And because you don't know what it is, is no proof that I don't know what it is. Let me go on.

The Soul Before and After Death

Now life here being sensation communicated to the soul through its physical mechanism, what are we to think of life before and after? When I say before, you instantly think of reincarnation. But do not be misled by phrases which you do not understand. What I am telling you is not reincarnation, about which I say nothing, but the pre-existence of the soul. All souls are eternal, being parts of the Divine Essence.

For reasons known to Him who is over all, it is deemed essential that the soul should be passed through the training of physical life. It is part of the process by which the soul attains its ultimate evolution. The soul may have been incarnate before. The law is absolute but infinitely various.

(Here the writing broke off.)

Appendix

Notes on the Open door to the Open Secret

1. BY THE TRANSMITTER

After receiving the foregoing message. I hesitated for some time as to the right course to adopt. The statement, so precise, so positive, and yet so marvellous, seemed too astounding to be published even on the authority of Julia. In such matters I usually take counsel with Mrs. Besant; but Mrs. Besant is in the United States. I therefore sent proofs of the communication just as it was received to Mr. Leadbeater, to whom Mrs. Besant told me I could refer any questions upon which I wanted advice in her absence, and who is well known as the author of the remarkable papers, entitled *Invisible Helpers*. I also sent a proof to Mr. G. H. Lock, of Hull, who for years past has made a profound study of things occult, approaching them, not from the Theosophical, but from the Swedenborgian standpoint. In sending the proof, I simply asked them for their opinions as to whether they thought there was anything in it, as I rather shrank from the responsibility of publishing a statement so portentous unless I was encouraged so to do by those who had paid much more attention to such subjects than in my busy life I have ever found time to do. I append their replies.

2. BY A THEOSOPHICAL EXPERT

Mr. Leadbeater wrote as follows: Thank you for sending me the proofs of Julia's last letters. Her statements appear to me to be perfectly accurate, and I should have no doubt at all that the results she describes could be attained along the lines which she indicates. You would probably obtain such results almost immediately, but I should say that to gain the necessary control of thought would take the average business man very much longer than he would be at all likely to devote to the attempt. I agree with much that Julia says, though if I had myself been giving such advice I should have insisted more strongly upon the necessity of the experimenter's subjecting himself to severe moral training first of all, in order that he may not make an improper use of his powers when he acquires them. But I suppose she takes this for granted. Could you ask her to add a word of emphatic caution as to the terrible fate awaiting those who attempt to gain such powers for evil ends?

Also, I think what she says about absolute passivity may be misunderstood. I know perfectly what she means, but I doubt whether that is the best word to use. It may be taken to signify the condition of a medium – a mere instrument whose wires may be swept by any passing wind; whereas her meaning is rather that a man should hold his mind perfectly still, while his consciousness, keenly alert and watchful functions in that which lies beyond and higher than the mind. She shows this by remarking that even in the state of passivity the thought must be steadily concentrated, and the heart and soul must go out in a definite longing.

I have been taught to attach more importance than

she does to celibacy, vegetarianism, and abstinence from alcohol. I quite admit that it is undoubtedly a man's duty to keep his body in health; but I think he should control and use it – not allow himself to be dominated by its cravings. And I fear that, unless a man had developed his moral nature and obtained perfect command over his desires and passions – unless he were absolutely pure in heart and mind – there would be great danger of his falling before the temptation to use these astral powers for selfish ends, and so degenerating into what is called in the East black magic. The methods suggested are accurate enough, and much of the advice is very good; but I do think that much more stress ought to be laid upon the imperative necessity of the moral qualifications.

3. BY A DISCIPLE OF SWEDENBORG

Mr. Lock's Reply

With reference to the paper submitted to me, there are two points on which I think it incorrect. The first:

This about *difference of focus* is inaccurate, except as regards spirits in astral (elementary physical) bodies, or lowest-plane doubles. No change in optical focus could make a pure spirit visible.

I do not believe in this "perpetual supervision" in the sense suggested by Julia. Good spirits quickly get out of their astral plane, leaving the riff-raff, with whom association is not desirable. Under normal conditions, spirits are as unconscious of our presence as we are of theirs; for this depends upon the planal difference in the substances which compose the two kinds of bodies.

The rest of the paper seems to me quite right, and I

am very glad to see so much insistence upon the importance of never losing control of your faculties.

Potentially, we are all clairvoyant. But the whole social conditions are against the development of the faculty. Then, also, constitution has much to do with it, as I am absolutely certain. Those born under passive signs of the Zodiac, as Cancer, Pisces, and Virgo (this latter your own), are much more psychically susceptible than others. [Your ruling planet is in Cancer; and six out of the nine planets in your horoscope are in passive signs. Hence you have some capacity in this direction.]

As to the rest – all this is nothing new, and is perfectly correct. It is knowledge that has been handed down the ages by Rosicrucians and others, and expressed in different forms. I already possess – have long possessed – the clear statement of these processes, together with much that Julia has not told you. It is to all intents and purposes the process adopted by "self-developed" mediums. It is in part the "Yoga" practised by Theosophists. Julia has expressed the truth in the simplest and least objectionable form. You need have not the slightest objection to publishing it – nor the slightest fear. Moreover, one thing is quite certain; the few who attempt the process will not all succeed; the conditions of life are against it. Some few, who might thereby become useful, may be waiting for this very information.

Here was confirmation and encouragement indeed, after receiving which I decided to publish Julia's message, leaving it to my readers to verify for themselves the accuracy of the statement which she has made. I have not yet had time to make the experiment. When I have leisure and opportunity I shall put the matter to the test.

I hope any of my readers who try the experiment will keep me advised as to their results.

Julia's Reply

After receiving these communications from Mr. Leadbeater, I asked Julia what she thought of it. She replied as follows:

1. To Mr. Leadbeater

With regard to Mr. Leadbeater's caution, I think my message is better left as it is, and I think he will agree with me when I have finished. There is nothing gained by advertising dangers that you feel are too attractive. Personally I do not think that the danger referred to is so great. That it is real, I do not doubt, and you know there is truth in the possibility, but these things are under the control of a higher power. The opportunity to materialize Doubles is not one that is given to mankind without limit; it is permitted by the higher powers, but it is not a power that any one can make use of. You know how anxious I am for the highest life, and how sad I should be if anything was said that would deprave or degrade; but I don't think the warning necessary.

"If you put in Mr. Leadbeater's warning, you must say that I have always recognized that there are great dangers in the communion with the invisibles, and that if any one thinks to hold such communion for any purpose which he would be ashamed to acknowledge before all men, he had better not seek it, for it will be open before the eyes of all hereafter, as it is now to the eyes of spirits. That is all I need say as to that.

"I do not deny that the practice of asceticism may, after the practice is a custom, help the manifestation, but any physical privation that reminds you of physical existence entails more loss than gain.

2. To Mr. Lock

With regard to the criticisms of Mr. Lock, she wrote:

About the focus – I think I understand what his point of objection is. And to an extent I agree with him. But I think that while I made the statement too absolute, as it was universal, his would narrow the truth too much. For instance, there is no focus in the strict sense which would reveal the Invisibles to the eye of the mind. Yet there is a detachment of the mind, from the material, which enables it to become sensibly conscious of the existence of spirits embodied or disembodied which were before invisible.

While I do not deny that there are many things hidden from our eyes; we have far greater range of vision than you. I remember when I first dropped my body, this addition of the faculty of seeing spirits among men was something new and superadded to what I had before seen. I have not lost that gift, but rather extended it. I feel a difficulty in explaining how the law operates. But of this you may be quite sure. Your lives are open to the eyes of those invisible spirits who are permitted to see what you think and hear what you say. You are compassed about by a far greater company of witnesses than you imagine. They – but why try to persuade, when soon you will see for yourself?

No, I don't think that he is right about the communications being possible only from lower levels. We find such a difficulty in making you understand that we are not conditioned by your limitations. Where I am there is life, and a life that has love as its vital breath. That Divine thing can and does survive the difficulties of communicating with persons still on earth. But you need not go to Borderland for analogies. If your saints and sages can hold converse without loss of holiness or wisdom with savages and fools, why cannot we? There is more difference of plane between a good man and a bad man than there is caused by the accident of embodiment or disembodiment.

The Companions of the Rosary

"What I want you to do, if you find an opportunity," wrote Julia on September 27, 1896 "is to modernize the Rosary." "I don't think you can do better," she wrote on September 26, 1897, "than to have the list prepared (1) of persons and (2) of causes to whom and to which you are in some relation. Go through them all seriatim every morning before you begin your daily work, thinking, What can I do for this? What ought I to do? And when you finish jot down for your guidance any suggestion that may have occurred to you. The exercise will be most helpful."

This use of the meditation-moment is strongly insisted upon by Julia in the chapters "How to Widen the Chinks."

By way of helping to carry out this idea, I have bound up with these "Letters" several pages of ruled paper on which may be written a list of persons and of causes to whom and to which the reader may be in some relation. Such a list kept constantly at hand and regularly conned before the day's work begins would serve the purpose of a modernized Rosary. But it is not only in the early morning hour that it is well to run over in thought the names of those who have at one time or another entered into our lives. When waiting to keep an appointment, when traveling, or when sleepless at night, the practice of going over one by one the Companions of our Rosary will be most helpful. For as Julia says:

"Your success depends upon individualizing. Take each in turn. Think – a loving thought is a prayer. You have not time to pray? Then make time to think of those you love. Without thinking on to people you lose vital connection with them. For love dies when you never think of the person loved."

In a Rosary there are divisions or sections convenient for aiding the memory. When I was drawing up my own private Rosary, I found it very necessary to divide it into sections. There are first the members of the family into which you were born. Then come the members of the household which you have created and all the branches. After these two great sections of blood relations come the various categories of friends or foes, neighbors, dependents, or superiors. I found it most convenient to mark off these sections chronologically. There were, for instance, those amidst whom I grew up as a boy. Then came my school mates, then those with whom I served my apprenticeship, and so forth. There is the section of those whom you have been in love with and the section of those with whom you have been at feud. Then there are the categories arranged according to their geographical grouping, or their relation to various departments of life. There is the psychic group, the religious group, the philanthropic, and so forth. There is the section devoted to Russians and that devoted to Americans, and so forth.

All those who have in any way by sympathy or

antipathy come into direct human personal contact with our lives form in a very real sense a part of our lives. If Julia's suggestion of a modernized Rosary were carried out as a part of the daily ordering of our lives, it is obvious that the flood of loving thoughts which is the heart's blood of the divine life in man, would be enormously swollen, and human relationship would feel in every nerve the quickening stimulus of sympathy and affection.

Until we begin to draw up such a list, we have no idea of the extent to which we have allowed what were once healthy, helpful, friendly relations to be atrophied by neglect. The mere compiling of a list of Companions of the Rosary is useful, even if it is never used as Julia suggests. But if her advice is carried out and the long list of those who have mingled their lives with ours is scanned, however hurriedly, before the morning meal, who can estimate the means of grace, which thereby would be opened up to mankind?

For as Julia says, "What is the cause of most of the sadness of the world? Not poverty of this world's wealth, but poverty of loving thought."

And to all the Companions of the Rosary I commend her Message concerning our duties to our friends.

"If you can do nothing else, think of them lovingly; for the loving thought of a friend is an Angel of God sent to carry a benediction to the soul."

WILLIAM T. STEAD

Also available from
White Crow Books

Marcus Aurelius—*Meditations*
ISBN 978-1-907355-20-2

Elsa Barker—*Letters from
a Living Dead Man*
ISBN 978-1-907355-83-7

Elsa Barker—*War Letters
from the Living Dead Man*
ISBN 978-1-907355-85-1

Elsa Barker—*Last Letters
from the Living Dead Man*
ISBN 978-1-907355-87-5

Richard Maurice Bucke—
Cosmic Consciousness
ISBN 978-1-907355-10-3

G. K. Chesterton—*The
Everlasting Man*
ISBN 978-1-907355-03-5

G. K. Chesterton—*Heretics*
ISBN 978-1-907355-02-8

G. K. Chesterton—*Orthodoxy*
ISBN 978-1-907355-01-1

Arthur Conan Doyle—*The
Edge of the Unknown*
ISBN 978-1-907355-14-1

Arthur Conan Doyle—
The New Revelation
ISBN 978-1-907355-12-7

Arthur Conan Doyle—
The Vital Message
ISBN 978-1-907355-13-4

Arthur Conan Doyle with
Simon Parke—*Conversations
with Arthur Conan Doyle*
ISBN 978-1-907355-80-6

Leon Denis with Arthur Conan
Doyle—*The Mystery of Joan of Arc*
ISBN 978-1-907355-17-2

The Earl of Dunraven—
*Experiences in Spiritualism
with D. D. Home*
ISBN 978-1-907355-93-6

Meister Eckhart with Simon
Parke—*Conversations
with Meister Eckhart*
ISBN 978-1-907355-18-9

Kahlil Gibran—*The Forerunner*
ISBN 978-1-907355-06-6

Kahlil Gibran—*The Madman*
ISBN 978-1-907355-05-9

Kahlil Gibran—*The Prophet*
ISBN 978-1-907355-04-2

Kahlil Gibran—*Sand and Foam*
ISBN 978-1-907355-07-3

Kahlil Gibran—*Jesus
the Son of Man*
ISBN 978-1-907355-08-0

Kahlil Gibran—*Spiritual World*
ISBN 978-1-907355-09-7

Hermann Hesse—*Siddhartha*
ISBN 978-1-907355-31-8

D. D. Home—*Incidents
in my Life Part 1*
ISBN 978-1-907355-15-8

Mme. Dunglas Home; edited,
with an Introduction, by Sir
Arthur Conan Doyle—*D. D.
Home: His Life and Mission*
ISBN 978-1-907355-16-5

Andrew Lang—*The Book
of Dreams and Ghosts*
ISBN 978-1-907355-97-4

Edward C. Randall—
Frontiers of the Afterlife
ISBN 978-1-907355-30-1

Lucius Annaeus
Seneca—*On Benefits*
ISBN 978-1-907355-19-6

Rebecca Ruter Springer—*Intra
Muros: My Dream of Heaven*
ISBN 978-1-907355-11-0

W. T. Stead—*After Death*
or *Letters from Julia: A
Personal Narrative*
ISBN 978-1-907355-89-9

Leo Tolstoy, edited by Simon
Parke—*Tolstoy's Forbidden Words*
ISBN 978-1-907355-00-4

Leo Tolstoy—*A Confession*
ISBN 978-1-907355-24-0

Leo Tolstoy—*The Gospel in Brief*
ISBN 978-1-907355-22-6

Leo Tolstoy—*The Kingdom
of God is Within You*
ISBN 978-1-907355-27-1

Leo Tolstoy—*My Religion:
What I Believe*
ISBN 978-1-907355-23-3

Leo Tolstoy—*On Life*
ISBN 978-1-907355-91-2

Leo Tolstoy—*Twenty-three Tales*
ISBN 978-1-907355-29-5

Leo Tolstoy—*What is
Religion and other writings*
ISBN 978-1-907355-28-8

Leo Tolstoy—*Work While
Ye Have the Light*
ISBN 978-1-907355-26-4

Leo Tolstoy with Simon Parke—
Conversations with Tolstoy
ISBN 978-1-907355-25-7

Howard Williams with an
Introduction by Leo Tolstoy—*The
Ethics of Diet: An Anthology
of Vegetarian Thought*
ISBN 978-1-907355-21-9

**All titles available as eBooks, and select titles available in
Audiobook format from www.whitecrowbooks.com**